AF190982

E. U. Deuker

On the Way to a
Grammar of Free Musical Speech

A Pentatonic Approach to Improvisation

E. U. Deuker

On the Way to a
Grammar of Free Musical Speech

A Pentatonic Approach to Improvisation

FSC
www.fsc.org
MIX
Papier aus ver-
antwortungsvollen
Quellen
Paper from
responsible sources
FSC® C105338

Publishing and production: BoD – Books on Demand,
Norderstedt, Germany
Copyright 2016 by E. U. Deuker
Illustrations, Cover Painting by Gabo, Berlin
Editing by Cody Jolly
Layout by Martins Logins
Last minute edits by Barbara McLaughlan and Elita Saliņa
Last minute layout help by Beate Breustedt
All rights reserved
Including the right of reproduction
In whole or in part in any form
ISBN 978-3-8423-6963-4

Content

Preface

The human arts can be considered a second form of human language, which is still in development. However, it does not reflect our so-called 'reality', as our usual languages consisting of words do. This 'artistic language' reflects the content of our mind, if anything at all; its feelings, moods, fantasies, daydreams, and surreal creations of all kinds.

In the case of music, most musicians today are still in a position where they use this cultural language rather awkwardly. Modern musical performance mainly consists of the interpretation of written pieces or those learned by heart. If compared with our everyday languages, this amounts to the reading, or quoting, of fixed and prepared texts.

Improvisation in musical performance is what could be considered as something like free musical speech. Over the last 100 years, jazz has developed this way of 'speaking extempore' most profoundly and consistently. In jazz we find improvisational interpretations of given pieces, which is comparable to the relation of stories in a free, personal way; also, since the days of the 1960's free jazz, we find something like spontaneous musical conversations without a fixed content. In the beginning, these conversations were rather abstract, perhaps somewhat similar to modern sound poetry, as we find it in Dada and post-Dada literature. However, today we already find attempts to assimilate harmonic structures, in an intuitive way, into these 'conversations' to express oneself spontaneously through the music.

Searching for something like a grammar of the musical language, I find myself at a bit of a loss. Today, most jazz musicians seem to use the so-called 'scale theory' as a theoretical guide in what they do, but I would hesitate to compare this theory to the grammar of a language. It seems to me rather like a huge collection of recipes, without anything resembling a systematic skeleton.

In this book I would like to explore the possibilities of achieving such a grammatical system of the musical language.

Introduction

These notes are intended to be a practical guide to improvisation using pentatonic scales, and their hexatonic extensions, in most situations.

I address this book to readers with some basic musical knowledge; however, many basic musical concepts will be found in the appendices.
Talking about the language of music, it seems to me that the 'alphabet' of this language should be composed rather from pentatonic scales than from scales containing more notes (7, sometimes 6, or even 8). I hope I will be able to show why.
One word to the readers who already have some improvisational experience: Perhaps the best way for you to use this book is to study some of the examples at the end of the book first; look up the suggested pentatonic scales (and/or their hexatonic extensions) in chapter 5, try them out, and decide for yourselves if the pentatonic approach looks promising or not.
 A pentatonic scale can be any 5-note scale, with one restriction: It should be contained in one of a certain number of scales which I call 'cnc scales' or 'complete, non-chromatic scales'. These will turn out to be the modern standard scales of jazz improvisation.
There are many different possibilities to define such pentatonic scales. One example of which is the well-known pentatonic blues scale.

$$I - {}^bIII - IV - V - {}^bVII \, ,$$

$$\text{or, using } I = B^b\text{:} \quad B^b - D^b - E^b - F - A^b.$$

Another example is a scale of the following form:

$$I - {}^bIII - {}^bIV - {}^bV - {}^bVI$$

or, using $I = G$: G - B^b – B - D^b - E^b

At first glance, the latter scale seems to be highly artificial. Yet examining it more closely, we see that it is the arpeggio of the chord $B+\Delta^7$:

$$B - E^b - G - B^b$$

(the well- defined 3rd degree of Ab melodic minor) with the addition of D^b to create the 5-note-chord $B+\Delta^{79}$.

Let's just stick to this chord for a moment. If we add even another note, F, we come up with the consistent sounding (if played against the contemplated chord – try it out!) 6-note-scale.

$$G – B^b – B – D^b – E^b - F,$$

We can interpret this in several different ways:

1) It is identical with the chord $B+\Delta^{7/9/\#11}$.

2) It is identical with the A^b **melodic minor scale**, short of one note, the root A^b.

3) It is identical with a pentatonic scale that I will call 'B^b **diminished pentatonic**' (short: B^bd), of the form I - ^bIII - IV - V - VI, plus the note ^bII:

$$I \quad ^bII \quad ^bIII \quad IV \quad V \quad VI$$

$$B^b \quad B \quad D^b \quad E^b \quad F \quad G,$$

that is, a hexatonic (6-note) extension of B^bd.

Introduction
_____

This situation is a good example of what I would like to achieve in this book about improvisation. I want to provide the improviser with a practical tool for his or her choice of which notes to play, in which harmonic situations. In my opinion, the general use of pentatonic scales of different forms (and their hexatonic extensions) has several advantages when compared to other methods of improvisation.
For example, thinking in:

1) terms of the (arpeggiated) chords of a given progression; the traditional 'vertical' approach used by the early Dixieland and New Orleans Jazz improvisers.

2) terms of the, nowadays very frequently used, 'scale theory' of contemporary jazz improvisation.

Why?

Roughly spoken, I think that approach (1) employs too few notes (namely, the 4 chord notes), and approach (2) too many notes (the 7 notes of a scale, that includes the 4 chord notes). This creates some problems, practical ones in (1), it limits the musical language and is at the same time extremely hard to apply to quickly changing chord progressions, and theoretical ones in (2), there seem to pop up so-called 'avoid notes' everywhere. For example, if the underlying chord is GΔ^7 and the suggested scale is the corresponding major scale with the 'avoid note' **C**, the **4**th degree, which somehow doesn't sound 'good'. As a result, the scale theory also has a didactic problem. Learning improvisers are supposed to know 7 notes by heart in each situation, **and** additionally keep in mind which of those 7 notes they are **not** allowed to use. Obviously, they would be much better off if they were just taught the 6 notes which they should use.
George Russell, in his famous and influential 'Lydian Chromatic' approach, tries to solve the problem by suggesting the use (in the example above) of the **raised 4**th **C**# instead. This is a possible solution; however, to my ears, it is not an entirely convincing one.
What I try to show here is that 5-note, pentatonic scales and their 6-note, hexatonic extensions are the optimal sets of notes in most improvisational situations. They seem to be the characteristic notes that define the

musical flavour and mood, and should therefore be used as the 'skeleton' of the improvisation. Moreover, I hope to be able to show that the transitions from one pentatonic scale to the next come quite natural in the musical flow and are easy to learn (which does not mean, of course, that learning and practising them would not afford a considerable amount of work).

One last observation before I start. These considerations have their root in jazz theory and practice, which seems natural since jazz, as I already mentioned, is the musical style which investigated improvisation over the last 100 years more profoundly than any other. The results, however, are applicable to other musical realms as well. For this reason I have included not only jazz standards in the examples at the end of the book, but also standards from rock, tango, chanson, and other genres.

CNC-Scales

In this chapter I try to get a glimpse of the inner structure of the musical universe.

But in order to do so, it is inevitable to employ a certain level of abstraction. As a musician keen on practicing and getting practical tools for improvisation at hand, you might feel the impulse to skip this chapter – which you can do, if you like, and return to it later, in case I refer to it in later chapters in a way you don't understand. -

The starting point of our journey into the realms of music will be the traditional 12-element-set of tones, denoted by letters as usual, the **chromatic scale:**

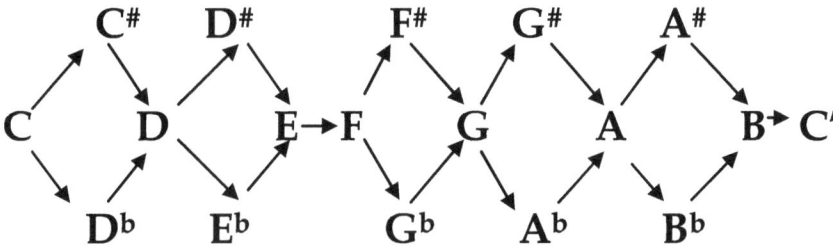

I guess you are familiar with the concept: the middle line of this diagram is the usual **C- ('melodic'-,** as we will call it) **-major scale**

$$ \text{C} \quad \text{D} \quad \text{EF} \quad \text{G} \quad \text{A} \quad \text{BC}' $$

with half steps **(h.s.)** between **E/F** and **B/C',** the upper and lower line give the 2 alternative names of the notes between the whole steps **(w.s.)** of the scale.

By way of the arrows we ordered our set of tones, corresponding to the pitch they have if played on an instrument; that is, the pitch of each tone to the right of an arrow is a h.s. higher than that of the tone to its left.

By way of counting the arrows between any two tones we can tell how many h.s. they are apart – f.i., C' is 12 h.s., or 'the interval of one octave', higher than C.

Strictly spoken, the chromatic scale continues to the right and also contains the notes C#' = Db', D'..., all of them an octave higher than their namesakes C# = Db, D... ; and in much the same way it continues to the left with notes of lower pitches. But for our considerations here, we reduce this potentially infinite set to the 12-element-set _above by considering their elements C, C#, D... as being representatives of all the low- and high-pitch Cs, C#s, Ds our ears can still identify as distinct tones when played on an instrument. You must only bear in mind that, when we speak about, say, the **A melodic major scale ('Amma'),** then we write it in the usual way

Amma: A   B   C# D   E   F# G# ,

but to be correct we would have to write it in this way, f.i.:

Amma: A   B   C#' D'   E'   F#' G#'

in order to make sure that the pitch order is the usual one we would have if we played the scale on an instrument; that is, f.e., the pitch of E' is higher than that of A (while actually the pitch of E is lower than that of A). –

Now, **scales**, in a very general way, are just **subsets of this chromatic scale**. They may contain any amount of elements, from 1 to 12.

I would like to define certain rules for the construction of scales, rules that give us just the scales that are 'meaningful' or 'of a certain flavour' in an intuitive way, like the familiar (to some of our readers, at least) 12 melodic/harmonic minor/major scales, the augmented and diminished scales; ruling out chromatic or partly chromatic scales, that is, scales that are 'too dense'.

To be precise, I will give now definitions for these intuitively important scales. In order to do so, we need the technical tool of 'scale degrees'. Scale degrees are, at first sight, nothing but new names for the 12 notes of our chromatic scale, and look like this:

CNC-Scales

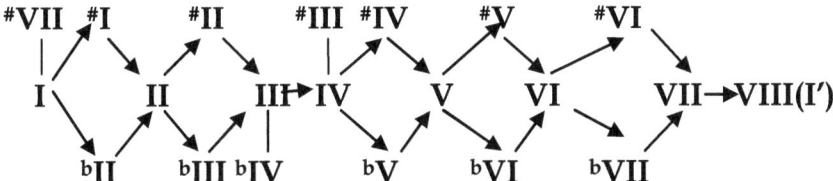

Much the same way as with the concrete notes, many scale degrees have 2 different names, #VII being the same degree as I, etc.

The concept of scale degrees is basically an abstraction: we introduce the Roman numbers as variables, and 'I' may now stand for C, but also for any of the other 11 notes C#, D,... If I = C, then, f. i., IV = F, #V = G#, etc.; but if I = A, then IV = D, #V = F, etc. In this way we will be able to compare scales of different sizes to each other. If you are not lucky with this abstraction, you can always switch to the familiar letters in your mind: insert C for I, D♭ for ♭II etc. We should realize that the letters themselves are already an abstraction: the C on a trumpet is not the same note as the C on a piano, f.i.

The degrees of any given scale can be denoted in different ways: take the 4-note-scale G – B♭ – C – D, for example. We might denote G = I; then the scale degrees would be

$$I - {}^{\flat}III - IV - V.$$

But we might as well denote G = V', which would give us

$$V' - {}^{\flat}VII' - I' - II'$$

with I = V', ♭III = ♭VII', IV = I', and V = II'.

We will call such a change of degree names a **renumeration** of the scale. As we see, such a renumeration leaves the **relative interval structure** of the scale unchanged. By this term we mean the sequel of the intervals between the scale notes. In our example, I - ♭III is a **min 3rd**; ♭III – IV a **w.s.**; IV – V also a **w.s.**; finally, V – I a **4th**. So the relative interval structure of I - ♭III - IV - V (and also of V' – ♭VII' – I' – II') is

$$\textbf{min 3}^{\text{rd}} - \textbf{w.s.} - \textbf{w.s.} - \textbf{4}^{\text{th}}.$$

(For those who are unfamiliar with intervals, we will define them later

on, step by step.) -
And now, to the definition of our scales:
The **'melodic major scale'** (**Imma**) is a **7-note scale** consisting of **w.s.**, except for 2 positions: between scale degrees **III** and **IV** and between **VII** and **VIII** (=**I**) we have **h.s.**
Explicitly, we have this sequence of scale degrees:

$$I \quad II \quad III \quad IV \quad V \quad VI \quad VII$$

This scale is synonymous with the traditional major scale.
From **Imma** we derive the **'melodic minor scale'** (**Immi**) by one alteration: it is of the form

$$I \quad II \quad {}^{\flat}III \quad IV \quad V \quad VI \quad VII \, ;$$

thus the **h.s.** are between **II** and **♭III** and **VII** – **I**.
Note: it is a classical custom to use this scale for upward-moving melodies, but the so-called **'natural minor'** scale (**Inmi**),

$$I \quad II \quad {}^{\flat}III \quad IV \quad V \quad {}^{\flat}VI \quad {}^{\flat}VII \, ,$$

in the same situation for downward-moving melodies. – This rule does not make sense in modern improvisation: the average improvisation line does not move upward or downward, it is a sequel of intervals with instantly chosen directions. Wherever we use this scale, **we leave its relative interval structure unchanged, in opposition to the classical definition.**
Moreover, there is no reason to introduce **Inmi** in our concept, as it is easily seen that it is identical with **♭IIImma**.

From **Imma** we derive the **'harmonic minor scale'** (**Ihmi**) by another alteration: its form is

$$I \quad II \quad {}^{\flat}III \quad IV \quad V \quad {}^{\flat}VI \quad VII \, .$$

Here we have **h.s.** between II – ᵇIII, V – ᵇVI **and** VII – I, as well as an **augmented step** (**a.s.;** equal to a **w.s.** plus a **h.s.**) between ᵇVI and VII. The '**harmonic major scale' (Ihma)**, again with the same root, alters ᵇIII back to III; thus we have

$$\text{I} \quad \text{II} \quad \text{III} \quad \text{IV} \quad \text{V} \quad \text{ᵇVI} \quad \text{VII} \,,$$

which amounts to **h.s.** between III – IV, V – ᵇVI, and VII – VIII, and an **a.s.** between ᵇVI and VII.
The '**diminished scale' (Idim)** is of this form:

$$\text{I} \quad \text{II} \quad \text{ᵇIII} \quad \text{IV} \quad \text{ᵇV} \quad \text{#V} \quad \text{VI} \quad \text{VII}$$

Here the **Vth** degree appears 2 times, as ᵇV and as #V, which might seem a little awkward. It is due to the fact that we actually have 8 notes in this scale, instead of 7 as in the former scales. – To introduce 8 scale degrees instead of 7 would be no amendment: the diminished scale would look better (I II III IV V VI VII VIII), but now we would have problems to represent our 7-tone-scales in an agreeable way.
We will stick to the tradition and represent all scales as alterations of the (melodic) major scale.
In the diminished scale we have alternating w.s. and h.s.: **w.s.** between I – II, ᵇIII – IV, ᵇV – #V, and VI – VII; **h.s.** between II –ᵇIII, IV – ᵇV, #V – VI, and VII – VIII.

Lastly, the '**augmented scales'**. Here we have 2 possible forms:

$$\textbf{(1)} \quad \text{I} \quad \text{II} \quad \text{III} \quad \text{#IV} \quad \text{#V} \quad \text{ᵇVII}$$

and

$$\textbf{(2)} \quad \text{I} \quad \text{#II} \quad \text{III} \quad \text{V} \quad \text{ᵇVI} \quad \text{VII} \,.$$

In the first form scale degree **VI**, in the second scale degree **IV**, doesn't appear at all – due to the fact that we want to present all scales as alterations of the melodic major scale, and the augmented scales consist only of 6 notes, instead of 7.
Scale (1) does not contain h.s. at all, only 6 w.s.; scale (2), on the contrary,

does not contain any w.s., only h.s. and a.s. (3 of each).

In order to distinguish these 2 forms we call (1) **Iaug(wt)** and (2) **Iaug(hta)**, wt denoting 'whole-tone' and hta denoting 'half-tone/augmented'.

It is important to note that of the **four 7-note-scales Imma, Immi, Ihma, Ihmi** there exist **12 different scales**, respectively, one for each of the possible roots C, D♭,...,B♭, B; while there are **only 3 different diminished** and **6 different augmented scales**.

This is due to the fact that of the 12 definable diminished scales, as a quick check will assure you, the 4 scales **Cdim, E♭dim, G♭dim** and **Adim**, are all actually identical, as well as the 4 scales **D♭dim, Edim, Gdim, B♭dim**, and the 4 scales **Ddim, Fdim, A♭dim, Bdim;** so the 3 different diminished scales are

C/E♭/G♭/Adim, D♭/E/G/B♭dim, and D/F/A♭/Bdim

In the sequel, we will call the 3 different scales by only one of its names – **Cdim** or one of the other 3, and likewise with the others. In the same fashion we will procede with their abstract names: the scale **I/♭III/♭V/VIdim** will shortly be called **Idim**, or **♭IIIdim...;** and likewise with the others.

In the case of the augmented scales, of the 12 defineable **Iaug(wt)**-scales the 6 scales **Caug(wt), Daug(wt), Eaug(wt), F#aug(wt), G#aug(wt), A#aug(wt)** are actually identical, as well as the 6 scales **C#aug(wt), D#aug(wt), Faug(wt), Gaug(wt), Aaug(wt), Baug(wt);** and of the 12 defineable **Iaug(hta)**-scales the 3 scales **Caug(hta), Eaug(hta),** and **A♭aug(hta)** are identical, and the same holds true for the 3 scales **D♭/F/Aaug(hta), D/G♭/B♭aug(hta),** and **E♭/G/Baug(hta)**, respectively.

This gives us the 2 aug(wt)-scales

C/D/E/F#/G#/A#aug(wt) and D♭/E♭/F/G/A/Baug(wt)

and the 4 aug(hta)-scales

C/E/A♭aug(hta), D♭/F/Aaug(hta), D/G♭/B♭aug(hta), and E♭/G/Baug(hta),

that is, 6 augmented scales, altogether. Analogously to the diminished

CNC-Scales

scales, we will call them shortly by the name of one of their representatives.

These, all in all, **57 different scales** (4x12 mma/mmi/hma/hmi-, 3 diminished, and 6 augmented scales) are the only ones that will occupy our mind from now on (still an impressive number, though!).

My goal is now to show that exactly these scales are 'perfect' in a certain sense, that is, neither too dense nor too small – they are **maximal** in the sense that they are not contained in another scale consisting of more tones.

In order to do so, I shall now define the above-mentioned rules for the construction of such perfect scales. To be precise, we will call them **'cnc-scales'** - 'cnc' standing for 'complete, non-chromatic'.

The rules are these:

1)   A cnc-scale does not contain 2 consecutive half-steps, and

2)   it is supposed to be maximal in the sense that it is not possible to add an additional note without violating rule 1.

Rule 1 is the reason why we call these scales 'non-chromatic', and rule 2 defines the completeness of the scales.

Now, it is quite easy to see that our **cnc-scales contain only h.s., w.s., or a.s.**

Indeed, consider any interval bigger than an a.s. in a given scale, and presume there is no other note of the scale embedded in this interval. Let **I** be the first note of the interval (a renumeration might be necessary), then its second note is further away from it than **III**. Consequently it is also further away from **II** than a w.s. - thus we can insert **II** at once without violating rule 1, **II** being in a 'safe distance' from both **I** and **III** and thus also from the 2nd note of the interval. This shows us our scale is not maximal in the sense of rule 2.

It also follows at once that in the case of an a.s. (or **'gap'**, as we also will call this interval from now on), that it must be **'genuine'**, or **'framed by 2 h.s.'**: let **I** - **#II** be the gap, thus it must necessarily continue to both sides: **VII** - **I** - **#II** - **III**. Suppose it were instead framed to the left by an interval bigger than a h.s., for example by the w.s. ♭**VII** – **I**. We could then insert #**I** between **I** and #**II**, giving us ♭**VII** – **I** – #**I** – #**II** – **III**, without contradicting rule 1. Similarly, if the gap were framed to the right by an interval bigger than a h.s., say by the w.s. #**II** - #**III**, we could fill in **II**. Consequently, the scale is not maximal in the sense of rule 2.

Now take for example the **A harmonic minor scale:** the a.s. here is the interval **F-G#**. It is genuine, because it is framed by the 2 h.s. **E** - **F** and **G#** - **A**. On the other hand, take the sequence **F-A♭-B♭-C-D-E**. This is no cnc-scale in our sense: the gap **F-A♭** can be filled by adding **G**, giving us the scale **Fmmi.** It is easy to see that all our 57 scales fulfil our rules and thus are really cnc-scales in the way we defined them; and a mathematician should not have great difficulties to show us that these are the only existing cnc-scales.

In the sequel I would like to outline such a proof – if you are not interested in such a matter, you can as well skip the rest of the chapter.

Now let us first consider all scales consisting of **7 notes, not containing any a.s.** Then we consequently have exactly **5 w.s.** and **2 h.s.**: 6 w.s. would already fill the octave (= **12 h.s.**), leaving no space for any h.s.; while, on the other hand, **3 h.s.** would leave just the space required for **3 w.s.** plus **one a.s. (3x1+3x2+1x3=12)** – which is exactly the situation of the harmonic scales (major and minor).

Let us still ask what possible positions those 2 h.s. could take in a given 7-note-scale: if we start the scale with a h.s., that is, **I** - ♭**II**, then rule 1 requires that the next step must be whole: **I** - ♭**II** - ♭**III**, while the next step could be the second h.s.. In this case we come up with this **'situation 1'**:

$$\text{sit.1:} \qquad I - {}^{\flat}II - {}^{\flat}III - {}^{\flat}IV - {}^{\flat}V - {}^{\flat}VI - {}^{\flat}VII$$

The second possibility would be a scale (**'situation 2'**) with the second h.s. between **IV** and ♭**V**:

$$\text{sit.2:} \qquad I - {}^{\flat}II - {}^{\flat}III - IV - {}^{\flat}V - {}^{\flat}VII - {}^{\flat}VII,$$

and that's it already: because the situation I - ^{b}II - ^{b}III - IV - V - VI - VII (the second h.s. between **VII** and **I**) contradicts rule 1, and the 2 situations left:

sit.3:   I - ^{b}II - ^{b}III - IV - V - ^{b}VI - VII

(second h.s. between **V** and ^{b}**VI**), and

sit.4:   I - ^{b}II - ^{b}III - IV - V - VI - ^{b}VII

(second h.s. between **VI** and ^{b}**VII**)_are identical with situations 1 and 2 respectively, as a simple renumeration shows: if we renumerate in sit. 1 **I** as **VI′**, then consequently ^{b}**II** is renumerated as ^{b}**VII′** etc., and we obtain the scale

$$VI' - {}^bVII' - I' - {}^bII' - {}^bIII' - IV' - V' ,$$

or

$$I' - {}^bII' - {}^bIII' - IV' - V' - VI' - {}^bVII'$$

which is identical with that of sit. 4 . - you can see at once that the argument also holds true for sit. 2 and 3 (renumerating in sit. 2 **I** as **V′**).
It is easy to see that all mmi-scales are of the form of sit.1, while all mma-scales are described by sit.2. –

Now let us consider **7-note-scales that do contain a.s.** Then we know already that this a.s. must be framed by 2 h.s. Now we might presume that there even follows a second a.s., which would give us the situation

$$VII - I - {}^\#II - III - V - {}^bVI .$$

As we see at once, this provides us automatically with a third a.s. ^{b}**VI** - **VII,** and the scale is already complete, and identical with the scale **VIIaug(hta)** - which contains only 6 notes. Thus, there are no 7-note scales containing 2 a.s.

Thus, the only possibility to complete the situation above is this:

$$VII - I - ^{\#}II - III - ^{b}V \ .$$

This can be continued in 2 ways:

$$1) \quad VII - I - ^{\#}II - III - ^{b}V - V$$

and

$$2) \quad VII - I - ^{\#}II - III - ^{b}V - ^{b}VI \ .$$

In case 1) we obtain as the only possible completion the scale
$$VII - I - ^{\#}II - III - ^{b}V - V - V.$$

By renumeration (**III = I′**) we obtain

$$V' - {}^{b}VI' - VII' - I' - II' - {}^{b}III' - IV' \ ,$$

which is identical with **I′hmi.**

In case 2) the only possible completion is the addition of **VI**, which renders
$$VII - I - ^{\#}II - III - ^{b}V - ^{b}VI - VI \ ,$$

and this scale (after the renumeration **III = I′**) is identical with

$$V' - {}^{b}VI' - VII' - I' - II' - III' - IV' \ ,$$

or **I′hma.**

Thus we have seen that a 7-note-scale with an a.s. is always identical with one of the scales **Ihmi** or **Ihma.** -

Next, we consider all scales consisting of 8 or more notes.

It is quite easy to see, then, that it can contain neither augmented steps nor 2 consecutive whole steps. Consequently, all whole steps that it contains must be framed on either side by half steps, and thus it must be necessarily of the form

I - II - ♭III - IV - ♭V - ♭VI - VI - VII,

with w.s. between I and II, ♭III and IV, ♭V and ♭VI, and between VI and VII; and h.s. between the remaining positions. - Especially it cannot contain more than 8 notes. -

To see that the assumption holds true we first consider all scales containing a.s. and show that they cannot contain more than 7 notes. Indeed, let's take the a.s. to be I - #II. As it must be framed by h.s., it continues thus to both sides:

VII - I - #II - III .

Now we see at once it cannot be continued by a second a.s. Indeed, consider, for example, ♭VI - I - VII - #II - III . Here, between III and ♭VI, 4 h.s. are left - but these should be covered by 3 notes if there were 8, all in all (the sequel already consists of 5 notes) - an impossible thing to do without contradicting rule 1.

Thus the sequel must be continued with a w.s. to both sides, rendering

VI - VII - I - #II - III - #IV .

Between #IV and VI, 3 h.s. are left - so there can be 'squeezed in' no more than 1 more note, without contradicting rule 1 - either V or #V. Thus the scale can consist of only 7 notes if it contains an a.s

Which leaves us to consider the case of 2 consecutive w.s. If there are 2 such, there might be even 3:

I - II - III - #IV.

These 4 notes cover 6 h.s., leaving 6 more h.s. to be covered by the remaining 4 notes. The only way to distribute 6 h.s. on 4 notes is to have the distances of 2 w.s and 2 h.s. between them.

One of the 2 w.s. might follow #IV - we then have

I - II - III - #IV - #V .

Then the next step is necessarily a h.s. - another w.s. would render us

I -II - III - #IV - #V - bVII, the 6-note-scale **Iaug(wt)**.

So we have now

$$\text{I - II - III - }^{\#}\text{IV - }^{\#}\text{V - VI .}$$

Between **VI** and **I** there can be squeezed only **VII** - rendering us a 7-note-scale. - Thus, the possibility of 3 consecutive w.s. is ruled out. Consequently we can only have

$$\text{I - II - III - IV ,}$$

which gives us immediately

$$\text{I - II - III - IV - V ,}$$

because of the h.s. between III and IV. - There are 2 possibilities to continue this sequel:

and

$$\textbf{1) I - II - III - IV - V - }^{b}\textbf{VI}$$

$$\textbf{2) I - II - III - IV - V - VI .}$$

In both cases, as is easily seen, it is not possible to 'squeeze' 2 more notes between bVI an I or VI and I without contradicting rule 1.

This completes the proof that all 8-note-scales are identical with one of the 3 diminished scales.

It remains to show that any scale with (at most) 6 notes is identical with one of the augmented scales (all containing 6 notes). - then, as a by-product, we obtain the result that no cnc-scale contains less than 6 notes. - Indeed: either it contains no h.s. - then it cannot contain any a.s. either, because, as we saw, an a.s. must be framed by 2 h.s. Thus in this case it contains only w.s. - and there must be 6 of them to fill the octave, so that it must necessarily be identical with one of the 2 aug(wt)-scales.

Or it does contain h.s. Then it must also contain a.s. - the only possibility to fill an octave with 6 notes, all of them h.s. or w.s. apart, is with 6 w.s. - Let I -#II be this a.s.; then our scale contains the segment

$$\text{VII - I - }^\#\text{II - III} .$$

Suppose it to be continued by a w.s., that is, we have

$$\text{VII - I - }^\#\text{II - III - }^\flat\text{V} .$$

In this situation we can then insert either **V**, $^\flat$**VI**, or **VI** between $^\flat$**V** and **VII** and get a 6-element-set of notes . But in each of these cases, we can add one more note to obtain a larger scale (**VI** in the cases of **V** and $^\flat$**VI**, and $^\flat$**VI** in the case of **VI**), contradicting rule 2.

Thus, the segment above can only be continued by another a.s.:

$$\text{VII - I - }^\#\text{II - III - V - }^\flat\text{VI} .$$

But thus a third a.s., $^\flat$**VI** - **VII,** is automatically produced, and the scale is identical with one of the aug(hta)-scales.

This completes the proof.
- From our proof it is immediately clear that whatever subset of notes we consider, if they contain 5 elements or less, and satisfy rule 1, they can always be embedded in one of our cnc-scales. Indeed: it is no restriction to consider only 5-element-subsets, and since we showed that any cnc-scale has at least 6 notes, it must always be possible to add one more note to such a subset without violating rule 1. It might be possible to add 1, 2, or even 3 more notes in this way - and, according to the completeness of our cnc-scale system, the completed subset must then be equal to one of the cnc-scales.

For our improvisational purposes this means if we use any arbitrary subset with less than 5 elements satisfying rule 1 in improvisation, we can think of actually moving in a certain cnc-scale - and it is indeed useful to make oneself clear which scale this is, because it can be an interesting strategy to start an improvisation with, say, 3 notes, and in the course of the solo successively to add the rest of the scale. Consider, for example, an improvisation over the chord **D**^{47}**.** You could start your solo with just these 3 chord notes: **D, G,** and **C;** after a while you might add **E** and **F,** after another while, **A** and **B,** thus arriving at the full cnc-scale **Cmma;** you can even go back to the original 3 notes, then add **E**ᵇ and **B**ᵇ, then **F** and **A**ᵇ, which new scale turns out to be **E**ᵇ**mma,** another cnc-scale containing **D, G,** and **C.** You can think up other situations for yourself and practise them.

Chords

In the previous chapter we learned which scales can be of practical use for improvisation, melodic/harmonic, major/minor, and diminished/augmented scales.

In practice, however, we don't come across scales, but **chord progressions** (a sequence of different chords). The chords in these progressions are mostly constructed from thirds, and are **tetrachords** consisting of four notes. Sometimes, in more recent compositions, we also find three note chords (**triads**) constructed from fourths. If you are not familiar with intervals, note this:

A **third (3rd)** is the interval of 2 notes that are 2 steps apart. These may be 2 h.s. (**diminished 3rd**), a w.s. and a h.s. (**minor 3rd**), 2 w.s. (**major 3rd**), or a w.s and an a.s. (**augmented 3rd**).

We could also define a 'doubly augmented 3rd', consisting of two a.s., but this is of no practical use.

In short, we have these 4 types: **dim, min, maj,** and **aug 3rd.**

A **fifth (5th)** is the interval of 2 notes that are two 3rds apart. These two 3rds can be either a dim and a maj 3rd or 2 min 3rds (**diminished 5th**), a dim and an aug 3rd or a min and a maj 3rd (**perfect 5th**), or a dim and an aug 3rd or 2 maj 3rds (**augmented 5th**).

In short, we have these 3 types: **dim, perf,** and **aug 5th** .

A **fourth (4th)** is the interval between the 3rd and the 5th; either a maj 3rd plus a h.s. (**perfect 4th),** or plus a w.s. (**augmented 4th**). There is the theoretical possibility of defining a 'diminished 4th', which would be equal to the maj 3rd, but for our purposes we can disregard it.

So we have 2 types of 4ths: **perf,** and **aug 4th** .

The last interval for the moment to be defined is the **seventh (7th)**. A 7th is the interval of 2 notes that are a 5th plus a 3rd apart. Again, we won't regard dim or aug 3rds. Thus, the 7th can be either a dim 5th plus a min 3rd (**diminished 7th**), a dim 5th plus a maj 3rd, a perf 5th plus a min 3rd (**minor 7th**), a perf 5th plus a maj 3rd, an aug 5th plus a min 3rd (**major 7th**), or an aug 5th plus a maj 3rd (**augmented 7th**).

This provides us with 4 types of 7ths: **dim, min, maj,** and **aug 7th.**

Now we are able to define **12 different tetrachords, plus 2 triads,** that will play the role of **'eigenchords'** (see next chapter) of the cnc-scales we defined in the last chapter. They are all constructed of dim, min, maj, and aug 3rds; except the triads, which consist of perf and aug 4ths. In fact, there are many more possibilities for defining tetrachords in this way, 59 to be exact. However, some of them are just 'inversions' and the others can be defined as 'substitutions' of the 14 chords I'm going to pick out here. (See app. 4)

Here are the rules for the construction of these chords and their names:

The **first note** of the chord we call its **root**. This note lends its name to the whole chord (**A, Bb, B,...**).

The **second note** is, in the case of the **tetrachords**, a (min or maj) 3rd apart from the root. If it is a **min 3rd** apart, we add a **- sign** to the name of the chord (**A-, Bb-,...**), while **a maj 3rd leaves the chord name unchanged (A, Bb,...**). In the case of the **triads**, the second note is a perf 4th apart from the root, and a **4 will be added to the chord name**.

The **third note** is, in the case of the **tetrachords**, a dim, perf, or aug 5th apart from the root. **Regarding the name of the chord, a perf 5th leaves it unchanged** (either **A-, Bb-,...**, or A, Bb,...). A **dim 5th** may consist of 2 min 3rds or of a maj and a dim 3rd. **In the first case, we assign an 'o' to the chord name; in the second, a 'ø'. An aug 5th** we denote with a '+' sign in the chord name. In the case of the **triads**, the 3rd note is a perf (or aug) 4th apart from the second, that is, a min (or maj) 7th apart from the root, and we **add a '7' or 'Δ7' to the chord name.**

The **fourth note** of the **tetrachords** is a min or maj 3rd apart from the 5th, and consequently a dim, min, maj, or aug 7th. **As for the chord name, a dim or aug 7th leaves it unchanged, a min 7th we denote by a '7' in the chord name (A7, A-7, Ao7, Aø7, A+7, ...), and a maj 7th by 'Δ7' (AΔ7, A-Δ7, ...**).

1) the tetrachords

The preceding considerations provide us with 12 different tetrachord types, or tetrachord qualities, with 12 possible different roots (each of which we substitute, as in the case of the scales, by the scale degree I). These are:

Chords

1) Io: min + min + min 3rd = min 3rd, dim 5th, dim 7th

2)* Io^7: min + min + maj 3rd = min 3rd, dim 5th, min 7th

3) I-^{7}: min + maj + min 3rd = min 3rd, perf 5th, min 7th

4) I-Δ^7: min + maj + maj 3rd = min 3rd, perf 5th, maj 7th

5) I^7: maj + min + min 3rd = maj 3rd, perf 5th, min 7th

6) IΔ^7: maj + min + maj 3rd = maj 3rd, perf 5th, maj 7th

7) I+Δ^7: maj + maj + min 3rd = maj 3rd, aug 5th, maj 7th

8) I+: maj + maj + maj 3rd = maj 3rd, aug 5th, aug 7th

9) IoΔ^7: min + min + aug 3rd = min 3rd, dim 5th, maj 7th

10)* Iø^7: maj + dim + maj 3rd = maj 3rd, dim 5th, min 7th

11)* IøΔ^7: maj + dim + aug 3rd = maj 3rd, dim 5th, maj 7th

12) I+7: maj + maj + dim 3rd = maj 3rd, aug 5th, min 7th

Chords 1 – 8 consist only of min and maj 3^{rd}s. Chords 9 – 12 also contain dim and aug 3^{rd}s.

Chord 8, **I+**, plays a special role. Being basically a triad, the aug 7th just doubling the root, it does not define a genuine tetrachord quality like the other chords. Nevertheless, I included it in the list here, as it will have its own place among the eigenchords we will define in the next chapter.

*For the sake of clarity, we deviate here from the traditional way to denote these chords, which is **I-^{7b5}** for **Io^7**, **I^{7b5}** for **Iø^7**, and **IΔ^{7b5}** for **IøΔ^7**.

2) The triads

Since Miles Davis' influential album, 'Kind Of Blue', extensive use has been made of the so-called 'sus-chords', denoted by I^7sus4, in jazz improvisation.

There are several possibilities to define these chords.

One possibility is to define I^7sus4 as the chord I^7 (or I-^{7}) with the maj 3rd (or min 3rd) substituted by the 4th. It has the form $I - IV - V - {}^bVII$.

Another way to interpret this chord would be to disregard the 5th, which does not essentially contribute to the 'flavour' of the chord, and to consider it to be constructed from 4ths instead from the usual 3rds. That is, the chord $I - IV - {}^bVII$ would be considered a triad constructed from 2 consecutive perf 4ths. In this book, we will use this interpretation.

Obviously, if we allow the 4th to be either perfect or augmented, there are 4 possibilities to construct triads from them:

a) from 2 consecutive perf 4^{ths}
b) from a perf followed by an aug 4th
c) from an aug followed by a perf 4th
d) from 2 aug 4ths.

Only the cases a) and b) lead to the creation of 2 genuinely new chord qualities. The chord we obtain from c) is of the form I - #IV - VII. It is the same as $Io\Delta^7$ (or $I\emptyset\Delta^7$), only the min (or maj) 3rd is omitted. The chord we obtain from d) is nothing but the interval aug 4th with an octave added (I - #IV - VIII).

Thus we are left with **2 new chord qualities** to complete our list:

13) I^{47}: **perf + perf 4th = perf 4th – min 7th** (from a)

14) $I^4\Delta^7$: **perf + aug 4th = perf 4th – maj 7th** (from b)

With these 14 chord qualities, we will define the concept of 'eigenchords' in the next chapter.

Eigenchords* of CNC-Scales

The general idea is to produce tetrachords from cnc-scale notes. The construction is as follows. We start consecutively with each scale note as a root and add 3 notes, choosing the notes that are 2 steps ahead in the scale, respectively. The resulting chords will then consist of (min and maj) 3rds, and consequently take the form of one of the chords 1 - 8 of the previous chapter. Indeed, 2 notes of a cnc-scale that are 2 steps apart from each other always form min or maj 3rds. Rule 1 of these scales makes sure that 2 steps cannot both be h.s. and must consequently be at least a min 3rd, while rule 2 assures us that 2 steps cannot be bigger than a maj 3rd; they are either maximally two w.s., or an a.s. and a h.s.

Take the scale **Bmmi**, for example. Starting with the scale note **D** as a root, we come up with the chord **D – F# - A# - C#**, that is, **D+Δ⁷**:

Bmmi:	**B**	**C#**	**D**	**E**	**F#**	**G#**	**A#**	**(B**	**C#)**
	I	II	♭III	IV	V	VI	VII	VIII	IX
								(=I)	(=II)
D+Δ⁷:			D		F#		A#		C#

The diagram shows that **D+Δ⁷** is the chord with its root on scale degree **♭III**, so the chord can be represented in the 'semi-abstract' form:

$$\text{♭III - V - VII - IX} \quad \text{or} \quad \text{♭III - V - VII - II}.$$

If we take a further step of abstraction, denoting by **X** the scale degree of the chord root, and agreeing that **X+2 and X+4** denote the scale degrees 2 and 4 steps ahead of X, then this becomes the abstract form:

$$X - X+2 - X+4 - X+6$$

---

*'eigen' is a german word meaning 'own' ('eigenchords' = 'a scale's own chords'). I borrowed the word construction from physics, where wave phenomenons are explained with the help of the words 'eigenwaves' and 'eigenfunctions'.

Scale chords produced by the use of this formula we call **'eigenchords in
the strict sense'**. The reason is that we can find additional eigenchords
which are constructed differently, yet take one of the chord forms 1 – 8 of
the previous chapter. If we allow the 3rds that form the chords to be also
dim or aug 3rds, then we can find even more interesting eigenchords.

For example, consider the following diagram of the scale **Fhma** and some
of the eigenchords we can produce from it:

Fhma:	F	G	A	B^b	C	D^b	E	F	G
	I	II	III	IV	V	^{b}VI	VII	VIII (=I)	IX (=II)
A-^{7}:			A		C		E		G
A^7:			A			D^b	E		G
A+^{7}:			A			D^b		F	G

The first of the three chords in the diagram, **A-7**, is of the (semi-abstract)
form

$$\text{III} \quad \text{V} \quad \text{VII} \quad \text{II}$$

or the (abstract) form

$$X \quad X+2 \quad X+4 \quad X+6$$

and thus, according to our definition, an eigenchord in the strict sense.
The second chord, **A7**, takes the form

$$\text{III} \quad \text{bVI} \quad \text{VII} \quad \text{II}$$

or

Eigenchords of CNC-Scales

$$X \quad X+3 \quad X+4 \quad X+6 \, ,$$

while **A+7** is of the form

$$\text{III} \quad {}^{\flat}\text{VI} \quad \text{I} \quad \text{II}$$

or

$$X \quad X+3 \quad X+5 \quad X+6 \, .$$

Both **A7** and **A+7** are not eigenchords in the strict sense. However, as improvisers we are not going to neglect these chords, since they enlarge our possibilities of interpretation. (The disadvantage of this attitude is that we have to learn more stuff; the advantage is that once we have learned it, we will have greatly enriched our improvisational vocabulary.)

Now we are ready to list all the eigenchords of all our scales:

Imma:	$I\triangle^7$	$II\text{-}^7$	$III\text{-}^7$	$IV\triangle^7$ $IV\text{ø}^7$	V^7	$VI\text{-}^7$	$VIIo^7$
	$I^4\triangle^7$	II^{47}	III^{47}		V^{47}	VI^{47}	VII^{47}

Immi:	$I\text{-}\triangle^7$	$II\text{-}^7$	${}^{\flat}III\text{+}\triangle^7$ ${}^{\flat}III\text{ø}\triangle^7$	IV^7 $IV\text{ø}^7$	V^7 $V\text{+}^7$	VIo^7	$VIIo^7$ $VII\text{ø}^7$ $VII\text{+}^7$
	$I^4\triangle^7$	II^{47}			V^{47}	VI^{47}	

Ihma:

I	II	III	IV	V	VI	VII
$I\Delta^7$	IIo^7	$III\text{-}^7$	$IV\text{-}\Delta^7$	V^7	$\flat VI\text{+}\Delta^7$	$VIIo$
		III^7				
	IIo		IVo		$\flat VIo$	
			$IVo\Delta^7$		$\flat VIo\Delta^7$	
					$\flat VIø\Delta^7$	
$I\text{+}\Delta^7$		$III\text{+}^7$				
$I^4\Delta^7$	II^{47}			V^{47}		

Ihmi:

I	II	III	IV	V	VI	VII
$I\text{-}\Delta^7$	IIo^7	$\flat III\text{+}\Delta^7$	$IV\text{-}^7$	V^7	$\flat VI\Delta^7$	$VIIo$
					$\flat VI\text{-}\Delta^7$	
	IIo		IVo		$\flat VIo$	
			IVo^7		$\flat VIo\Delta^7$	
					$\flat VIø\Delta^7$	
				$V\text{+}^7$		$VII\text{+}$
$I^4\Delta^7$	II^{47}	$bIII^4\Delta^7$		V^{47}		

Idim:

I	II	bIII	IV	bV	#V	VI	VII
Io	IIo	$\flat IIIo$	IVo	$\flat Vo$	$\#Vo$	VIo	$VIIo$
Io^7	IIo^7	$\flat IIIo^7$	IVo^7	$\flat Vo^7$	$\#Vo^7$	VIo^7	$VIIo^7$
	$IIø^7$		$IVø^7$		$\#Vø^7$		$VIIø^7$
	$II\text{-}^7$		$IV\text{-}^7$		$\#V\text{-}^7$		$VII\text{-}^7$
	II^7		IV^7		$\#V^7$		VII^7
$I^4\Delta^7$		$bIII^4\Delta^7$		$bV^4\Delta^7$		$VI^4\Delta^7$	

Iaug(wt):

I	II	III	#IV	#V	bVII
$I\text{+}$	$II\text{+}$	$III\text{+}$	$\#IV\text{+}$	$\#V\text{+}$	$\flat VII\text{+}$
$Iø^7$	$IIø^7$	$IIIø^7$	$\#IVø^7$	$\#Vø^7$	$bVIIø^7$
$I\text{+}^7$	$II\text{+}^7$	$III\text{+}^7$	$\#IV\text{+}^7$	$\#V\text{+}^7$	$bVII\text{+}^7$

Eigenchords of CNC-Scales

Iaug(hta):	I+	#II+	III+	V+	bVI+	VII+
	I-Δ7		III-Δ7		bVI-Δ7	
	IΔ7		IIIΔ7		bVIΔ7	
	I+Δ7		III+Δ7		bVI+Δ7	

Notes and Comments:

- The first row of chords in each scale consists of strict eigenchords (**e.c.**), all others are additional e.c.

- We see that **Imma** produces 4 different strict and 3 different additional types of e.c., 7 from our list of 14 chord types in chap. 3. $X\Delta^7$ appears in 2 places, $X\text{-}^7$ in 3 places, and X^{47} even in 5 places. The others show up only in 1 place.

- **Immi**, on the other hand, produces 5 different strict and also 5 different additional e.c., 10 in all. X^7, $X\text{-}^7$, and $X\emptyset^7$ appear in 2 places, X^{47} in 3 places, and all others appear only once.

- It is interesting to note that the 7 strict e.c. of **Ihma** are exactly the first 7 chords from our list, and each shows up exactly once. Taking the additional e.c. into account, we have 13 from our list of 14 chord types. The only chord type not showing up at all being $X\emptyset^7$. X^7, Xo^7, and X^{47}, appear in 2 places, Xo, in 4, and all the others only once.

- Like with **Ihma,** the 7 strict e.c. of **Ihmi** are the first 7 chords from our list and each
shows up only once, but only X^7 and Xo^7 in the same places as in Ihma. Taking the additional e.c. into account, we have 13 from our list of 14 chord types here as well; again missing only $X\emptyset^7$. Of these chords, Xo^7, $X^{4}\Delta^7$, and X^{47} appear in 2 places, Xo in 4 places, and the rest only once.

- The diminished scale **Idim** produces just one strict e.c. type, Xo, which consequently appears in 8 different places, mirroring the symmetry of the scale. All in all, we have 5 different chord types here. Xo and Xo^7 appear in 8 places, and the other 3, $X\text{-}^7$, X^7, and $X\emptyset^7$, in 4 places.

- The scale **Iaug(wt)** produces one type of strict e.c., **X+**, and 2 other types of additional e.c., **X+^{7}** and **Xø^7**; all of which appear in 6 places.

- Lastly, **Iaug(hta)** produces the same type of strict e.c. as **Iaug(wt)**, **X+**, as well as 3 types of additional e.c., **X-Δ^7**, **XΔ^7**, and **X+Δ^7**. **X+** appears in 6 places, and the others each appear in 3 places.

The Types of Pentatonics We Will Use

In this chapter I concentrate on the development of the different types of pentatonics, starting with the well-known (and, I think, for most of the readers fairly familiar) Blues-(minor-)pentatonic. **A good strategy for reading and learning might be just to peruse this chapter now, then go on to the next chapter, and return here later for closer examination.**

The Blues-pentatonic is of this form:

$$\textbf{Ip:} \quad \text{I} \quad \text{^{b}III} \quad \text{IV} \quad \text{V} \quad \text{^{b}VII}$$

Often the note ^{b}V is included as well, which is a very reasonable thing to do, but for the moment we will leave all possible additional notes there are more of them) out. We will come back to them later.

Here I present the minor form of this pentatonic. In many books about jazz improvisation you will find the major form:

$$\text{I}' \quad \text{II}' \quad \text{III}' \quad \text{V}' \quad \text{VI}'$$

The relative interval structure of both scales are the same, that is, you can obtain one from the other by a transposition (VI'→I):

$$
\begin{array}{ccccc}
\text{VI}' & \text{I}' & \text{II}' & \text{III}' & \text{V}' \\
\updownarrow & \updownarrow & \updownarrow & \updownarrow & \updownarrow \\
\text{I} & {}^b\text{III} & \text{IV} & \text{V} & {}^b\text{VII}
\end{array}
$$

In other words, the **A-min-Blues-pentatonic** is identical with the **C-maj-Blues-pentatonic** and likewise. Each min-Blues-pentatonic is identical with the maj-Blues-pentatonic whose root is the min 3rd of said min-Blues-pentatonic.

For the presentation of my pentatonic concept, the min form of the Blues pentatonic is more convenient; so, I choose it as a starting point. We called it **Ip** above – the 'p' simply standing for 'pentatonic'.

In many cases it is convenient to have 'pentachord'-representations of the pentatonics we use. In the case of **Ip**, we compare **Ip** and **I-7**:

Ip:	I		^{b}III	IV	V		^{b}VII
I-7/11*:	1		^{b}3	11	5		7,

which shows us that **Ip** and the familiar tetrachord **I-7**, **11th** added, are identical:

$$\text{Ip} = \text{I-}^{7/11}.$$

The next type of pentatonic we obtain from **Ip** by altering one note. We diminish ^{b}**VII**, in order to obtain **VI**, and then have:

Id:	I	^{b}III	IV	V	VI

The 'd' in the scale name stands for 'diminished'.
In this case, we can compare **Id** with the pentachord **IV79**:

Id:	IV	VI	I	^{b}III	V
IV79 (IV = 1):	1	3	5	7	9,

this shows us that:

$$\text{Id} = \text{IV}^{79},$$

Id is identical with the dominant 7th chord **IV7**, with the 9th added. For example, if **I = D**, then **Dd = G79**.

By a further diminishment, namely V→^{b}V, we obtain the pentatonic:

*Here and in the following I make use of the usual interval notation in chords, see app. 2.

The Types of Pentatonics We Will Use

Io: **I**   **^{b}III**   **IV**   **bV**   **VI**

The 'o' in the scale name indicates the double diminishment.

Note that **Io** is identical with the pentachord **IV^{7b9}**:

Io:			**IV**	**VI**	**I**	**^{b}III**	**^{b}V**
IV^{7b9} (IV = 1):			1	3	5	7	^{b}9 ,

or

$$\text{Io} = \text{IV}^{7b9}$$

In other words, **Io** is identical with the same dominant 7th chord **IV^7** as **Id,** but with the 'altered note' b9 added.
Later on, we will use these 2 pentatonics, **Id** and **Io,** as the most frequent or the 'standard interpretations' of the dominant 7th chord.

For example, if we choose **I = E,** then **Eo = A^{7b9}**. In practice, it will usually be the other way around. You stumble on a dominant 7th chord; while searching for a pentatonic interpretation, you look up the 5th of the chord. This will be the root of the pentatonic you use. Say the chord is **B^7**, its 5th is **F$^{\#}$**; so, **F$^{\#}$d** or **F$^{\#}$o** will be your standard pentatonic interpretation of the chord.

There is an ambiguity of denotation here. With Io I already denoted the chord

I ^{b}III ^{b}V   VI

in chap. 3, but I don't think this will create any problems for the reader. From the context in which it is used, it should always be clear if **Io** is referring to the chord or the pentatonic scale.

By using another diminishment, $IV \to {}^bIV$, we obtain:

$$\textbf{Iobl:} \quad I \quad {}^bIII \quad {}^bIV \quad {}^bV \quad VI,$$

The 'bl' standing for 'Blues'. I chose this name to indicate the presence of both ${}^bIII$ and ${}^bIV$ = III (min and maj 3rd) here, which is a typical Blues feature.

The comparison:

Iobl:		bV	VI	I	bIII	bIV
${}^bV o^{7/13}$ (${}^bV = 1$):		1	b3	b5	13	7

renders the equation:

$$\textbf{Iobl} = {}^bV o^{7/13}$$

Choosing $I = G^b$, we see that $G^b obl = C o^{7/13}$.

Finally, by altering ${}^bIII \to III$ from **Id,** we obtain:

$$\textbf{Imd:} \quad I \quad III \quad IV \quad V \quad VI \;,$$

'md' standing for 'major diminished'.

Note that **Imd** is identical with the pentachord $IV\Delta^{79}$:

Imd :	IV	VI	I	III	V
$IV\Delta^{79}$:	1	3	5	$\Delta 7$	9

or

$$\textbf{Imd} = IV\Delta^{79} \text{ (or, equivalently, } \textbf{Vmd} = I\Delta^{79})$$

For example, if $I = D^b$, then $D^b md = G^b\Delta^{79}$.

The Types of Pentatonics We Will Use

In concrete improvisational contexts, it is often easier to think of **Imd** in terms of this pentachord, as we will see.

There are two more identities of **Imd** with other scales on the hexatonic level, which are worth mentioning:

$$\textbf{Imd(9) = IIp(9) = VIp(b13)} \text{ (see app. 5, p. 177, equ. 8)}$$

These may also be helpful in some contexts.

- Now that's it already!), with these relatively few pentatonics (only 5!) and some hexatonics derived from them, we are going to stand our improviser in every conceivable improvisational context! If that's not a promise…

This is really surprising, if you consider the fact that we have distinguished no less than 12 tetrachord (plus 2 triad) qualities. We should have expected that, by expanding them to 5-note-scales, we would come up with many more pentatonics! In fact, we could, but it is not necessary, as we will see.

Enlarging Our Pentatonics to Hexatonics, and Scales

In the following, we will see that our 5 types of pentatonics, via their hexatonic extensions, can generate all of our familiar cnc-scales; except for the augmented scales, which will be obtained directly from certain chords. (In fact, we would be free to decide to call the augmented scales 'hexatonics', as they consist of 6 notes, but I hesitate to do so, as there seems to be no agreeable way to define them as extensions of any pentatonic.)

To each of our 5 pentatonic types, there exist 4 or 5 hexatonic extensions (4 in the case of **Ip, Id,** and **Imd,** and 5 in the case of **Iobl** and **Io**). You can find the details in app. 5. There, I also discuss the fact that we do not consider all the hexatonic types when we want to enlarge our pentatonics to cnc-scales. You also find a **'shortcut list'** there about the relationships between pentatonics, hexatonics, and cnc-scales, which I repeat here:

Shortcut List

pentatonics   **hexatonic extensions**   **generated scales**

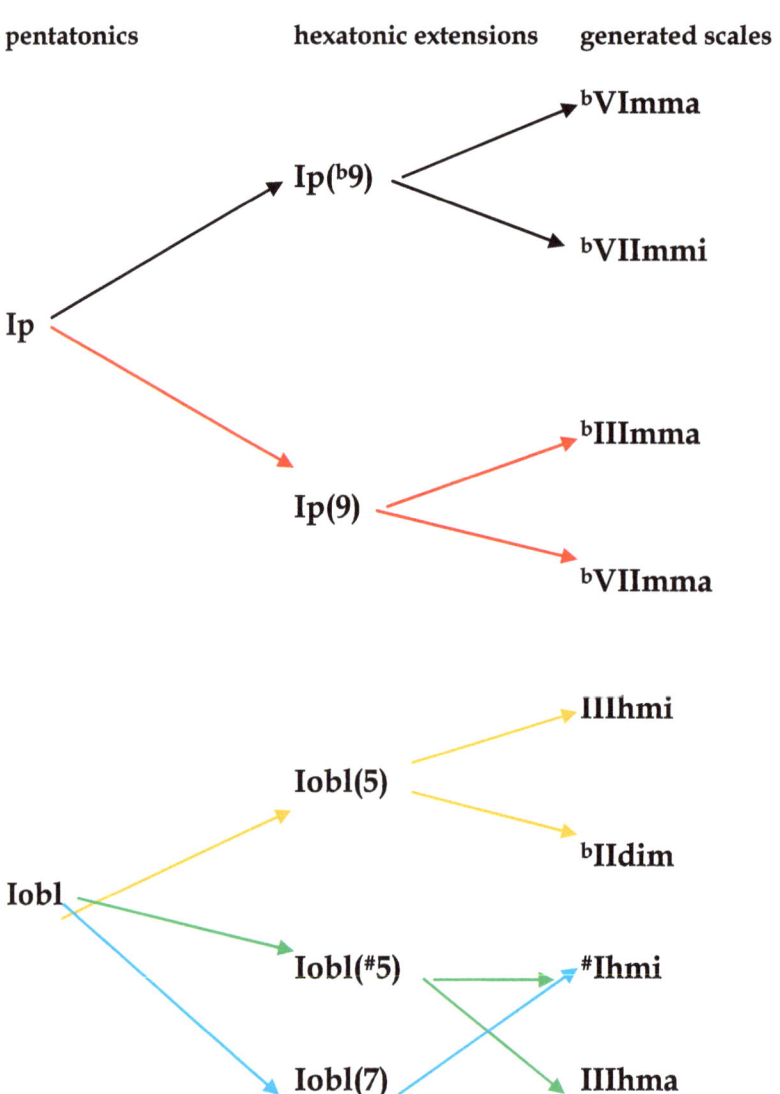

The Types of Pentatonics We Will Use

pentatonics   **hexatonic extensions**   **generated scales**

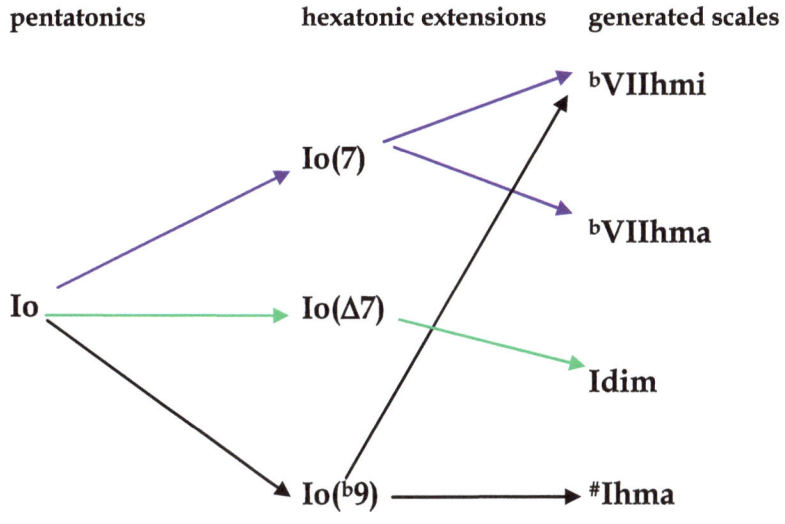

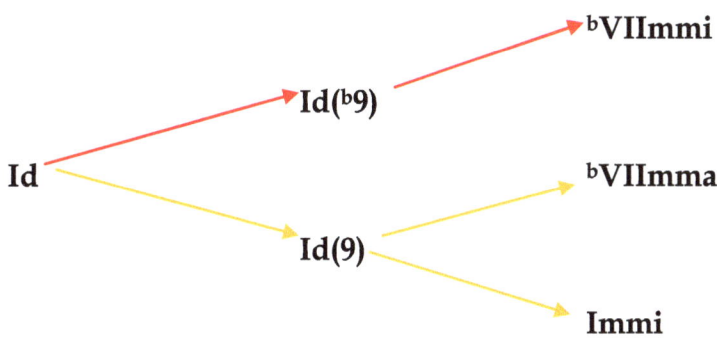

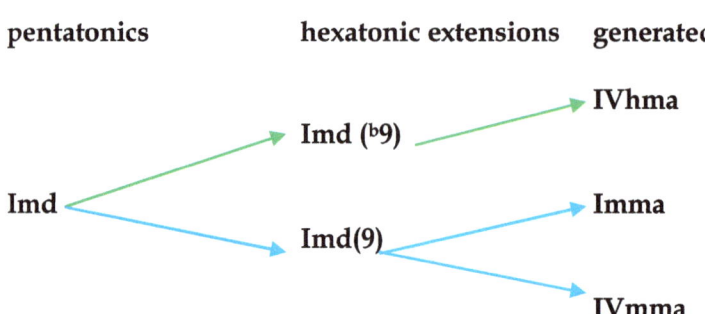

pentatonics   hexatonic extensions   generated scales

We see that, **with the exception of the augmented scales, all scale types can be generated by our 5 types of pentatonics**. This is even possible in more than one conceivable way (**Imma** by **IIp, IIIp, VIp, IId, Imd,** and **Vmd; Immi** by **IIp, Id,** and **IId; Ihma** by **ᵇVIobl, IIo, VIIo,** and **Vmd; Ihmi** by **ᵇVIobl, VIIobl,** and **IIo;** and **Idim** by **II/IV/ᵇVI/VIIobl** and **I/ᵇIII/ᵇV/VIo;** see app. 1).

A remark about denotation: In the definition of the hexatonic extensions of pentatonics, we used the same Arabic numbers for the intervals as in the definition of chords (see app. 2). For example, **Imd(9)** is the pentatonic **Imd** with a **II** added:

$$\textbf{Imd(9)} = \textbf{I} \;\; \textbf{II} \;\; \textbf{III} \;\; \textbf{IV} \;\; \textbf{V} \;\; \textbf{VI}.$$

Eigenscales

In chapter 4, we started with scales and listed their eigenchords. In this chapter we take a different view. We start with the chords and list the possible scales they might belong to. It is a bit like trees and landscapes. The trees are the chords, and the landscapes are the scales. You can consider them from different points of view. You can visit a certain landscape and look at what kinds of trees you find there, or you can climb a tree and try to recognize the kind of landscape that surrounds you. In this chapter we are going to take the second point of view.

While doing so, we go even a step further. As we called this book 'a pentatonic approach to improvisation', we will also take the pentatonic scales, as well as the hexatonics derived from them, into account here. Sticking with our metaphor (chords = trees, scales = landscapes), we can consider the pentatonics and hexatonics to be something like micro-climates. Just as trees generate different micro-climates, chords generate different pentatonics; which belong to even more different scales, as we will see.

So, let's now take our list of 14 different chord qualities from chap. 3, and list all of the pentatonic scales that can be generated from these chords. The second step will be to list all of the cnc-scales these pentatonics can generate.

In the following table, I list all 14 chord types obtained in chap. 3 and extend them into all possible pentatonics of the types I considered in chap. 5. Then I choose the corresponding hexatonic extensions and generated scales from the 'shortcut list' in that chapter.

Often enough, the chords will not be contained completely in a pentatonic, but only in a hexatonic extension of it. I will also include these hexatonics in my list.

In app. 5, we listed several equalities between hexatonics. Whenever 2 hexatonics are equal, you will only find one of them in the list.

- You may have noticed that this is the longest chapter of this book. This is due to my endeavour to list all scale extensions of our 14 chords as completely as possible. This is supposed to help the curious reader to find hitherto unknown scale combinations of his own invention. I will discuss the most common applications of these results in the following chapters.

1) Io

Io(chord):	**I**		**ᵇIII**			**ᵇV**		**VI**
Io(pent):	**I**		**ᵇIII**		**IV**	**ᵇV**		**VI**
(ᵇIIo:		ᵇII		III		#IV	V		ᵇVII)
(ᵇIIo(Δ⁷):	I	ᵇII		III		#IV	V		ᵇVII)
ᵇIIdim:	**I**	**ᵇII**	**ᵇIII**	**III**		**#IV**	**V**	**VI**	**ᵇVII**
Iobl:	**I**		**ᵇIII**	**ᵇIV**		**ᵇV**		**VI**	
(IImd:			II			#IV	V	VI	VII)
(IImd(ᵇ9):			II	ᵇIII		#IV	V	VI	VII)
Vhma:	**I**		**II**	**ᵇIII**		**#IV**	**V**	**VI**	**VII)**

pentatonics	hexatonic extensions	generated cnc-scales

Here, I put in brackets and wrote the pentatonics and hexatonics which do not themselves contain the whole chord, but only their extensions, in non-bold italics. I will proceed in the same way throughout the rest of the chapter.

The list presented here is not complete. Due to the symmetry of **Io**, it is not only contained in the pentatonics above (**Io** and **Iobl**), but also in their min-3ʳᵈ-relatives:

$$\mathbf{^bIII/^bV/VIo} \text{ and } \mathbf{^bIII/^bV/Vobl} \,.$$

So, in order to be complete, here is a list of all of the scales generated by **Io**:

$$^{♭}\text{II/III/V/}^{♭}\text{VIIhma/hmi, I/}^{♭}\text{IIdim}$$

Now, let us study a concrete example and let **I** be **C**. Then, **Co** generates the pentatonics **C/E♭/G♭/Ao,** (D♭/E/G/B♭o), **D♭/E/G/B♭obl,** (D/F/A♭/Bmd), and their extensions **D♭/E/G/B♭hma/hmi** and **C/D♭dim.**

2) Io^7

	I	♭II	II	♭III	III / ♭IV	IV	#IV / ♭V	V	♭VI	VI	♭VII	
Io⁷:	I			♭III			♭V				♭VII	
(Io:	I			♭III		IV	♭V			VI		)
Io(7):	I			♭III		IV	♭V			VI	♭VII	
(♭IIo:		♭II			III		#IV	V			♭VII	)
(♭IIo(Δ7):	I	♭II			III		#IV	V			♭VII	)
♭IIdim:	I	♭II		♭III	III		#IV	V		VI	♭VII	
(VIo:	I		II	♭III			♭V			VI		)
VIo(♭9):	I		II	♭III			♭V			VI	♭VII	
♭Vobl:	I			♭III			♭V			VI	♭VII	
(♭IId:		♭II			♭IV		♭V		♭VI		♭VII	)
(♭IId(9):		♭II		♭III	♭IV		♭V		♭VI		♭VII	)
♭IImmi:	I	♭II		♭III	♭IV		♭V		♭VI		♭VII	
♭IIId:	I			♭III			♭V		♭VI		♭VII	
(IVd:	I		II			IV			♭VI		♭VII	)
(IVd(♭9):	I		II			IV	♭V		♭VI		♭VII	)
♭IIImmi:	I		II	♭III		IV	♭V		♭VI		♭VII	

	I	bII	bIII	IV	bV	bVI	bVII	
(Io⁷:	I		bIII		bV		bVII	)
(bIImd:		bII		IV	bV	bVI	bVII	)
(bIImd(9):		bII	bIII	IV	bV	bVI	bVII	)
bIImma:		**bII**	**bIII**	**IV**	**bV**	**bVI**	**bVII**	
(IVmd:						bVI	bVII	)
(IVmd(b9):					bV	bVI	bVII	)
bVIImma:					**bV**	**bVI**	**bVII**	
(bVImd:		bII	bIII			bVI		)
(bVImd(9):		bII	bIII			bVI	bVII	)
(bIImma:		bII	bIII		bV	bVI	bVII	)*

pentatonics **hexatonic extensions** **generated cnc-scales**

(Io) ⟶ **Io(7)**
(bIIo) ⟶ (bIIo(Δ⁷)) ⟶ **bVIIhma**

(VIo) ⟶ **VIo(b9)**
bVobl ⟶ **bVobl(5)** ⟶ **bVIIhmi**
⟶ **bVobl(#5)**
⟶ **bVobl(7)** ⟶ **bIIdim**

(bIId) ⟶ (bIId(9))
bIIId ⟶ **bIIId(b9)** ⟶ **Vhmi**
⟶ **bIIId(9)**

(IVd) ⟶ (IVd(b9)) ⟶ **bIImmi**
(bIImd) ⟶ (bIImd(9))
(IVmd) ⟶ (IVmd(b9)) ⟶ **bIImma**
(bVImd) ⟶ (bVImd(9)) **bIIImmi**

* I put this scale in brackets as it is already contained in the list, as an extension of bIImd(9).

Of the o- and obl-pentatonics, the list above could actually even contain a few more. Namely, besides **bIIo(Δ^7)** and ^{b}**Vobl,** their respective min-3rd-relatives, **III/V/^{b}VIIo(Δ7), Iobl(7),** ^{b}**IIIobl(5), and VIobl(^{b}9)**. They are all contained in ^{b}**IIdim**.

Again, let's study a concrete example. Let **I** be **G,** then **Go^7** generates the 2 pentatonics **D^{b}obl** and **B^{b}d,** as well as the 2 hexatonics **Go(7)** and **Eo(^{b}9)**. These scales in turn generate **B^{b}d** (**A^{b}mma/mmi** and **B^{b}mmi**), **Fhma** (**Go(7),Eo(^{b}9)** and **D^{b}obl**), **Fhmi** (**Go(7)** and **D^{b}obl**), **Dhmi** (**Eo(^{b}9)** and **D^{b}obl**), and **A^{b}dim** (**D^{b}obl**).

3) I-⁷

	I	bII	II	bIII	bIV	IV	#IV	V	bVI	VI	bVII	
I-⁷:	I			**bIII**				**V**			**bVII**	
Ip:	I			**bIII**		IV		**V**			**bVII**	
(IIp:	I		II			IV		V		VI		)
(IIp(b9):	I		II	bIII		IV		V		VI		)
bVIImma:	I		**II**	**bIII**		IV		**V**		VI	**bVII**	
(Id:	I			bIII		IV		V		VI		)
Id(7):	I			bIII		IV		V		VI	bVII	
(bVIIo:		bII		bIII	bIV			V			bVII	)
(bVIIo(9)*:		**bII**		**bIII**	**bIV**			**V**			**bVII**	)
(VIo:	I		II	bIII			#IV			VI		)
(VIo(b9)**:	I		II	bIII			#IV			VI	bVII	)
Vhmi:	I		**II**	**bIII**			**#IV**	**V**		VI	**bVII**	
(bIIIobl:	I			bIII			#IV	V		VI		)
bIIIobl(5):	I			**bIII**			**#IV**	**V**		VI	**bVII**	
bIIImd:	I			**bIII**				**V**	**bVI**		**bVII**	

*Note that , besides the **min 3ʳᵈ** of the chord, **bIII,** this hexatonic also contains the **maj 3ʳᵈ, bIV = III.** Usually, this note is considered to be 'non-harmonic' in this context, a synonym for 'Do not use it!' To my ears, the use of this hexatonic, and of its extension **bIIdim,** makes perfect sense in this situation. Try it out for yourself.

Interestingly, this hexatonic has its root one h.s. below that of the former, **bVIIo(9). Both 'fit' the chord **I-⁷,** in the sense that **I-⁷** is contained in one of them (**bVIIo(9)**) and in the scale extension of the other (**Vhmi**). This is mirrored by the fact that **I-⁷** is both the eigenchord of the **3ʳᵈ degree** of **Vhmi,** as well as the **4ᵗʰ degree** of **bVIhma.**

	I	II	ᵇIII	IV	V	VI	ᵇVII	
I-⁷:	**I**		**ᵇIII**		**V**		**ᵇVII**	
(IVmd:	I	II		IV		VI	ᵇVII	)
(IVmd(9):	I	II		IV	V	VI	ᵇVII	)
(ᵇVIImma:	I	II	ᵇIII	IV	V	VI	ᵇVII	)
(ᵇVIImd:		II	ᵇIII	IV	V		ᵇVII	)
ᵇVIImd(9):	**I**	**II**	**ᵇIII**	**IV**	**V**		**ᵇVII**	

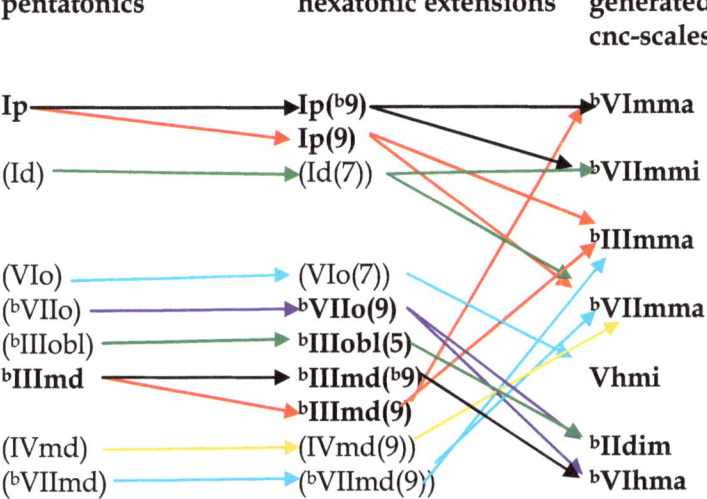

pentatonics   **hexatonic extensions**   **generated cnc-scales**

To illustrate these results for **I-⁷**, let us consider the case **I = F**. Then **F-⁷** generates the pentatonics **Fp** and **Aᵇmd**, as well as the additional hexatonics **Fd(7)**(which is identical with **Fp(13)**), **Eᵇo(9)**, and **Aᵇobl(5)**. The generated scales are **Dᵇmma** (**Fp** and **Aᵇmd**), **Eᵇmmi** (**Fp** and **Fd(7)**), **Aᵇmma** (**Fp** and **Aᵇmd**), **Eᵇmma** (**Fp**), **Chmi** (via **Do**), **Gᵇdim** (**Eo(9)** and **Aᵇobl(5)**), and **Dᵇhma** (**Eᵇo(9)** and **Aᵇmd**). **F-⁷** is an eigenchord of both **Chmi** and **Dᵇhma**, their roots being a h.s. apart.

4) I-Δ⁷

	I	II	♭III	IV	#IV	V	♭VI	VII
I-Δ⁷:	I		♭III			V		VII
(IIp:	I	II		IV		V	VI	)
(IIp(♭9):	I	II	♭III	IV		V	VI	)
Immi:	**I**	**II**	**♭III**	**IV**		**V**	**VI**	**VII**
(Id:	I		♭III	IV		V	VI	)
Id(Δ⁷):	I		♭III	IV		V	VI	VII
(IId:		II		IV		V	VI	VII)
(IId(♭9):		II	♭III	IV		V	VI	VII)
(Immi:	I	II	♭III	IV		V	VI	VII)
(IIo(♭9):		II		IV		V	♭VI	VII)
(IIo(♭9):		II	♭III	IV		V	♭VI	VII)
Ihmi:	**I**	**II**	**♭III**	**IV**		**V**	**♭VI**	**VII**
(#IVo:	I		♭III		#IV		VI	VII)
#IVo(♭9):	**I**		**♭III**		**#IV**	**V**	**VI**	**VII**
(VIo:	I	II	♭III		#IV		VI	)
(VIo(7):	I	II	♭III		#IV	V	VI	)
Vhma:	**I**	**II**	**♭III**		**#IV**	**V**	**VI**	**VII**
(VIIobl:		II	♭III	IV			♭VI	VII)
(VIIobl(♭9):	I	II	♭III	IV			♭VI	VII)
(Ihmi:	I	II	♭III	IV		V	♭VI	VII)
(IImd:		II			#IV	V	VI	VII)
(IImd(♭9):		II			#IV	V	VI	VII)
Vhma:	**I**	**II**	**♭III**		**#IV**	**V**	**VI**	**VII**
Iaug(hta):	**I**		**#II** III			**V**	**♭VI**	**VII**

Eigenscales

pentatonics	hexatonic extensions	generated cnc-scales
(IIp)	(IIp(♭9))	Immi
(Id)	Id(Δ^7)	
(IId)	((IId(♭9))	Ihmi
(IIo)	(IIo(♭9))	
(#IVo)	#IVo(♭9)	Vhma
(VIo)	(VIo(7))	
(VIIobl)	(VIIobl(♭9))	IIIhmi
(IImd)	(IImd(♭9))	
-	-	Iaug(hta)

Observe that **Iaug(hta)** contains **III**, the maj 3rd of **I-Δ^7**. Scale theorists would probably call this an 'avoid note'. Try out the sound of this scale for yourself.

As an example, let **I = B**. Then the chord **B-Δ^7** generates the hexatonics **Bd(Δ^7)** and **Fo (♭9)**, and the scales **Bmmi, Bhmi, G♭hma, E♭hmi,** and **Baug(hta)**.

5) I^7

	I	♭II	II	♭III	III/♭IV	IV	♯IV/♭V	V	VI	♭VII	
I^7:	I				III			V		♭VII	
(VIp:	I		II		III			V	VI		)
VIp(♭9):	I		II		III			V	VI	♭VII	
Vd:	I		II		III			V		♭VII	
(VId:	I		II		III		♯IV		VI		)
(VId(♭9):	I		II		III		♯IV		VI	♭VII	)
Vmmi:	I		II		III		♯IV	V	VI	♭VII	
(♭IIo:		♭II			III		♯IV	V		♭VII	)
♭IIo(Δ7):	I	♭II			III		♯IV	V		♭VII	
(IIIo:		♭II			III			V	VI	♭VII	)
IIIo(♯5):	I	♭II			III			V	VI	♭VII	
Vo:	I	♭II			III			V		♭VII	
(♭VIIo:		♭II		♭III	♭IV			V		♭VII	)
♭VIIo(9):	I	♭II		♭III	♭IV			V		♭VII	
(Iobl:	I			♭III	♭IV		♭V		VI		)
(Iobl(7):	I			♭III	♭IV		♭V		VI	♭VII	)
♭VIIdim*:	I	♭II		♭III	♭IV		♭V	V	VI	♭VII	
(♭IIobl:		♭II			III	IV		V		♭VII	)
(Iobl(7):	I			♭III	♭IV		♭V		VI	♭VII	)
♭VIIdim*:	I	♭II		♭III	♭IV		♭V	V	VI	♭VII	

*The min-3rd-relatives of **Iobl**, as well being part of **bVIIdim**, could also be included in this list.

Eigenscales

	I	bII	bIII	III/bIV	IV	V	bVI/VI	bVII	
I⁷:	I			III		V		bVII	
(bIIobl:		bII		III	IV	V		bVII	)
bIIobl(Δ⁷):	I	bII		III	IV	V		bVII	
(IIIobl:		bII		III		V	bVI	bVII	)
IIIobl(#5):	I	bII		III		V	bVI	bVII	
(Imd:	I			III	IV	V	VI		)
Imd(7):	I			III	IV	V	VI	bVII	
(bIIImd:	I		bIII			V	bVI	bVII	)
bIIImd(b9):	I		bIII	bIV		V	bVI	bVII	

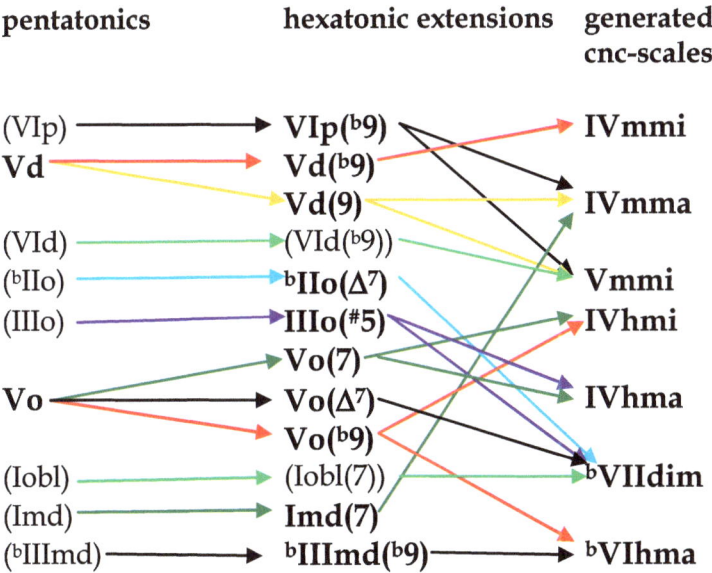

pentatonics	hexatonic extensions	generated cnc-scales

Equation 2 of app. 5 (p. 177) provides us with an **interesting additional scale**. It tells us that **Vo(b9),** one of the hexatonics above, is equal to **IIIobl(#5).** Comparing the two pentatonics

Vo:	I	^{b}II	III		V		^{b}VII	

IIIobl:		^{b}II	III		V	^{b}VI	^{b}VII	

shows us that **IIIobl,** contrary to **Vo**, does not contain the root of I^7, but all of its other notes. There is one scale extension of **IIIobl** that is not included in our list, as it also does not contain the root, but all other notes of I^7, **VIIdim:**

IIIobl:		^{b}II		III		V	^{b}VI	^{b}VII	

VIIdim:	$^\#$I	II	III	IV		V	^{b}VI	^{b}VII	VII

This scale can also be used for improvisation over I^7, and it has been used in the past (John Coltrane made extended use of it). Alternatively, try one of the hexatonics which are included in this scale, **IVo(Δ^7)**, ^{b}**VIo(Δ^7)**, ^{b}**IIobl(7)**, and **IIIobl(7)**.

Please note that this means we have the choice of 2 different diminished scales if we come across this chord, ^{b}**VIIdim** and **VIIdim**. I recommend to make use of this fact in improvisation by switching from one scale to the other. For example, in funk tunes like 'Freedom Jazz Dance' (see also p. 149 ff) where you often find lengthy passages in which the underlying I^7-chord does not change.

A special feature of **VIIdim** is that it contains simultaneously the **7** and the Δ^7 of I^7. This is interesting, because if you would like to think in terms of 'avoid notes' (as the 'scale theorists' do), then in the case of I^7, the Δ^7 would certainly be one. Try it out for yourself, to see if you like the sound of this scale in this situation.

In the case of ^{b}**VIIo**, the hexatonic extension ^{b}**VIIo(9)** contains 2 so-called 'altered notes', ^{b}**II** and ^{b}**III**, the ^{b}**9** and $^\#$**9** of the chord. The term 'altered' suggests that the 'normal' scale to be played on the chord would be

IVmma ($\mathbf{I}^7$ being its dominant 7th chord) which contains **II**, and that it is possible to 'alter' it into $^{\flat}\mathbf{II}$ or $^{\#}\mathbf{II}$ in improvisation, giving the chord a different sound. In the context of this book, however, there is no reason to consider **IVmma** to be something like the 'genuine' scale of this chord. It is just one of several choices (and not even the best one. We already discussed the problems aroused when using its root, **IV**, over $\mathbf{I}^7$).

In 'chord voicings' of $\mathbf{I}^7$ (the way you choose the pitch of the notes the chord consists of) often the 5th of the chord is omitted, as it does not define the flavour of it in the way the 3rd or the 7th do. It is too close to the root, being its third harmonic. (We could even call it 'the small octave', in a way.) The omission of the 5th creates the opportunity to add an **'altered 5th'** to the chord, the $^{\flat}5$ or the $^{\#}5$, in many situations. The resulting 'altered dominant 7th chords', $\mathbf{I\emptyset}^7$ and $\mathbf{I+}^7$, make it possible to use even more pentatonics and scales in improvisation (see the discussion of these chords below, under 9) and 10)).

As an example, let I be **D**. Then, $\mathbf{D}^7$ generates the pentatonics **Ad** and **Ao**, which provide us with the scales **Gmma, Gmmi, Ammi (Ad), B$^{\flat}$hma, Ghma, Ghmi,** and **E$^{\flat}$dim (Ao).** Additional hexatonics containing the chord are **Bp($^{\flat}$9), E$^{\flat}$o(Δ^7), F$^{\#}$o($^{\#}$5), Dmd(7),** and **Fmd($^{\flat}$9).** As an alternative to **E$^{\flat}$dim,** we can use **Edim** here as well.

6) IΔ7

	I	II/#II	III	IV/#IV	V	bVI/VI	VII
IΔ7:	I		III		V		VII
(IIo:		II		IV	V	bVI	VII)
(IIo(7):	I	II		IV	V	bVI	VII)
Ihma:	I	II	III	IV	V	bVI	VII
(#IVo:	I	#II		#IV		VI	VII)
(#IVo(7):	I	#II	III	#IV		VI	VII)
IIIhmi:	I	#II	III	#IV	V	VI	VII
(VIIo:		II	III	IV		bVI	VII)
(VIIo(b9):	I	II	III	IV		bVI	VII)
(Ihma:	I	II	III	IV	V	bVI	VII)
(#IIobl:	I	#II		#IV	V	VI	)
(#IIobl(b9):	I	#II	III	#IV	V	VI	)
(IIIhmi:	I	#II	III	#IV	V	VI	VII)
(Imd:	I		III	IV	V	VI	)
Imd(Δ7):	I		III	IV	V	VI	VII
(IImd:		II		#IV	V	VI	VII)
(IImd(9):		II	III	#IV	V	VI	VII)
Vmma:	I	II	III	#IV	V	VI	VII
Vmd:	I	II	III		V		VII
Iaug(hta):	I	#II	III		V	bVI	VII

Remember the identity **Vmd = IΔ79** (see chap. 5, p. 42).

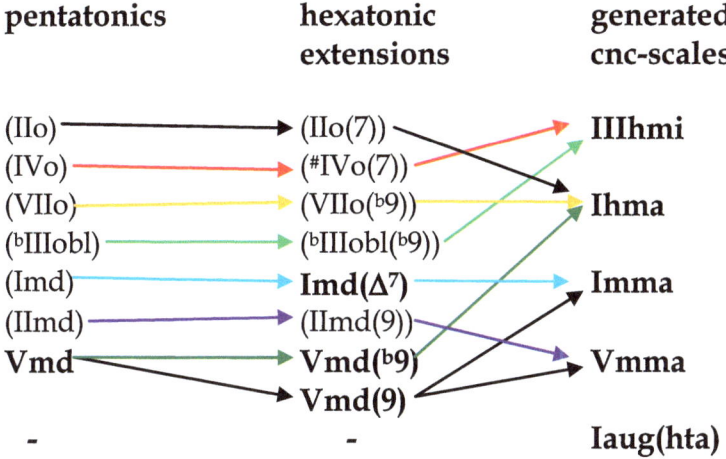

pentatonics	hexatonic extensions	generated cnc-scales

Let's choose B^b to be I. Then, $B^b\Delta^7$ generates the pentatonic **Fmd,** the hexatonic B^b**md(Δ^7),** the scale **Dhmi** (which we interpret as an extension of either **Eo** or D^b**obl),** and B^b**aug(hta). Fmd,** which is identical to $B^b\Delta^{79}$ (and also D-^{7b13}), generates the scales B^b**hma/mma** and **Fmma.**

7) I+Δ⁷

	I	II	III	#IV/IV	V	#V/ᵇVI	VI	VII
I+Δ⁷:	**I**		**III**			**#V**		**VII**
(VId:	I	II	III	#IV			VI	)
(VId(9):	I	II	III	#IV			VI	VII)
VImmi:	**I**	**II**	**III**	**#IV**		**#V**	**VI**	**VII**
(VIId:		II	III	#IV		#V		VII)
VIId(ᵇ9):	**I**	**II**	**III**	**#IV**		**#V**		**VII**
(#IIo:	I	#II		#IV		#V	VI	)
(#IIo(ᵇ9):	I	#II	III	#IV		#V	VI	)
IIIhma:	**I**	**#II**	**III**	**#IV**		**#V**	**VI**	**VII**
(#IVo:	I	#II		#IV			VI	VII)
(#IVo(9):	I	#II		#IV		#V	VI	VII)
(IIIhma:	I	#II	III	#IV		#V	VI	VII)
(VIIo:		II	III	IV		#V		VII)
VIIo(ᵇ9):	**I**	**II**	**III**	**IV**		**#V**		**VII**
(Vmd:	I	II	III		V			VII)
Vmd(ᵇ9):	**I**	**II**	**III**		**V**	**ᵇVI**		**VII**
(VIImd:		#II	III	#IV		#V		VII)
VIImd(ᵇ9):	**I**	**#II**	**III**	**#IV**		**#V**		**VII**
Iaug(hta):	**I**	**#II**	**III**		**V**	**ᵇVI**		**VII**

pentatonics	hexatonic extensions	generated cnc-scales
(VId) ———————→	(VId(9)) ——————→	VImmi
(VIId) ———————→	**VIId($^\flat$9)**	
(#IIo) ———————→	(#IIo($^\flat$9)) ————→	**IIIhma**
(#IVo) ———————→	(#IVo(9))	
(VIIo) ———————→	**VIIo($^\flat$9)**	
(Vmd) ———————→	**Vmd($^\flat$9)**	
(VIImd) ———————→	**VIImd($^\flat$9)**	
-	-	**Iaug(wt)**

Choosing $I = A^\flat$, the chord $A^\flat + \Delta^7$ generates the hexatonics **Gd/o/md($^\flat$9)** and $E^\flat$**md($^\flat$9)**, which can be extended to the scales **Fmmi (Gd), Fhmi (Go), A$^\flat$hma (Go and E$^\flat$md),** and **Bhma (Gmd). A$^\flat$aug(hta)** is obtained immediately from the chord.

- We leave **8)** out, as it did not denote a genuine new chord quality **(I+)**, and continue with **9)**.

9) Iø⁷

	I	bII	II	bIII	III	bIV	IV	#IV	bV	V	bVI	VI	bVII	
Iø⁷:	I				III				bV				bVII	
(**bIId:**		bII				bIV			bV		bVI		bVII	)
bIId(△⁷):	I	bII				bIV			bV		bVI		bVII	
(**bIIId:**	I			bIII					bV		bVI		bVII	)
bIIId(b9):	I			bIII		bIV			bV		bVI		bVII	
(**Vd:**	I		II		III					V			bVII	)
Vd(△⁷):	I		II		III			#IV		V			bVII	
(**VId:**	I		II		III				bV			VI		)
VId(b9):	I		II		III				bV			VI	bVII	
(**bIIo*:**		bII			III			#IV		V			bVII	)
bIIo(△⁷):	I	bII			III			#IV		V			bVII	
(**Iobl**:**	I			bIII		bIV			bV			VI		)
Iobl(7):	I			bIII		bIV			bV			VI	bVII	
Iaug(wt):	I		II		III				bV		bVI		bVII	

*Of the min-3ʳᵈ-relatives of **bIIo**, we have **IIIo(9)**, **Vo(△⁷)**, and **bVIIo(9)** all contained in **bIIdim.**

Of the min-3ʳᵈ-relatives of **Iobl, we have **bIIIobl(b9)**, **bVobl(7)**, and **VIobl(7)** again contained in **bIIdim.**

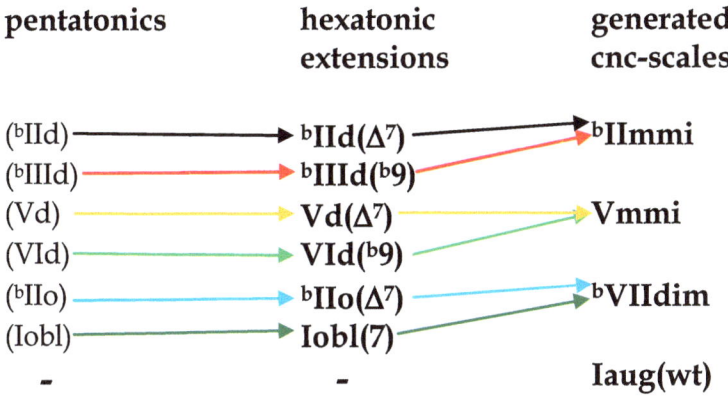

pentatonics	hexatonic extensions	generated cnc-scales
(^{b}IId)	^{b}IId(Δ^7)	^{b}IImmi
(^{b}IIId)	^{b}IIId(^{b}9)	
(Vd)	Vd(Δ^7)	Vmmi
(VId)	VId(^{b}9)	
(^{b}IIo)	^{b}IIo(Δ^7)	^{b}VIIdim
(Iobl)	Iobl(7)	
-	-	Iaug(wt)

$I\emptyset^7$ is one of the 'altered 7th-chords' we mentioned when we discussed I^7 in chord 5). One of the scales that it generates, ^{b}**IImmi,** is an important tool in improvisation:

^{b}**IImmi:**   I ^{b}II ^{b}III ^{b}IV ^{b}V ^{b}VI ^{b}VII

The scale contains all possible 'altered notes' you can play over the chord $I\emptyset^7$, ^{b}9 (^{b}II), $^\#$9 (^{b}III), ^{b}5 (^{b}V), and $^\#$5 (^{b}VI). The rest of the scale notes, I, ^{b}IV (=III), and ^{b}VII, form the chord I^7 without the 5th (V). As we mentioned under chord 5), in chord voicings of I^7 often the 5th is omitted, or substituted by ^{b}5, or $^\#$5. In both cases, as we see, ^{b}IImmi (called **'I superlocrian'** by the scale theorists) can be used in improvisation.

Note the symmetry of $I\emptyset^7$. It consists of 2 w.s. (**III - ^{b}V and ^{b}VII - I**) which are a maj 3rd apart:

$I\emptyset^7$: ^{b}**VII**   **I**   **III** ^{b}**V.**

With **I' = ^{b}V**, we get:

$$\text{I}'\text{ø}^7: \qquad {}^{\text{b}}\text{VII}' \qquad \text{I}' \qquad\qquad \text{III}' \qquad {}^{\text{b}}\text{V}'$$
$$\updownarrow \qquad\qquad \updownarrow \qquad\qquad \updownarrow \qquad\qquad\qquad \updownarrow \qquad\qquad \updownarrow$$
$$^{\text{b}}\text{V}\text{ø}^7: \qquad \text{III} \qquad {}^{\text{b}}\text{V} \qquad\qquad {}^{\text{b}}\text{VII} \qquad \text{I}$$

That is, $^{\text{b}}\text{Vø}^7$ consists of the same notes as Iø^7, the 2 chords are identical:

$$\text{Iø}^7 = {}^{\text{b}}\text{Vø}^7$$

For example, $\text{Eø}^7 = D\ E\ G^{\#}\ A^{\#} = A^{\text{b}}\ B^{\text{b}}\ D\ E = B^{\text{b}}\text{ø}^7$.

This relationship is reflected by the fact that both $^{\text{b}}\text{IImmi}$ and Vmmi are eigenscales of Iø^7. They are, in a way, 'anti-symmetric' to each other:

Iø^7:	I			III	^{b}V			^{b}VII
^{b}IImmi:	I	^{b}II		^{b}III	^{b}IV	^{b}V		^{b}VI	^{b}VII
Vmmi:	I		II	III	$^{\#}$IV	V		VI	^{b}VII

They are anti-symmetric in the sense that **the first part of** ^{b}**IImmi, I -** ^{b}**II -** ^{b}**III -** ^{b}**IV**, has the same relative interval structure as the second part of **Vmmi,** $^{\#}$**IV - V - VI -** ^{b}**VII** (h.s. – w.s. – h.s.) The same is true for **the** second part of the former (^{b}V - ^{b}VI - ^{b}VII) and the first part of the latter (I – II – III), w.s –w.s.

The symmetry goes even further. Consider the 2 other eigenscales of the chord:

Iø^7:	I			III	^{b}V			^{b}VII
^{b}VIIdim:	I	^{b}II		^{b}III	III	^{b}V	V	VI	^{b}VII
Iaug(wt):	I		II	III	^{b}V		^{b}VI	^{b}VII

We see that the 4 eigenscales of the chord show exactly the 4 possibilities to fill its gaps, **I –III** and ^bV - ^bVII.

$I\varnothing^7 = {}^bV\varnothing^7$ is the basis for a phenomenon called **'tritone substitution'** in **major II-V-I-progressions** (see p. 98).

- To illustrate these relations, we choose **I** = G^b. Then, $G^b\varnothing^7$ generates G^b**aug(wt)**, and the hexatonics **Gd(Δ^7), Ad($^b9$), D^bd(Δ^7), E^bd($^b9$), Go(Δ^7),** and G^b**obl(7)**. These, in turn, generate the scales **Gmmi (Gd** and **Ad), D^bmmi (D^bd** and **E^bd),** and **Gdim (Go** and G^b**obl).**

10) I+⁷

	I	bII	II	bIII	III	bIV	IV	bV	V	bVI / #V	bVII	
I+7:	I				III					#V	bVII	
(bIId:		bII				bIV		bV		bVI	bVII	)
bIId(Δ7):	I	bII				bIV		bV		bVI	bVII	
(bIIId:	I			bIII				bV		bVI	bVII	)
bIIId(b9):	I			bIII		bIV		bV		bVI	bVII	
(IVd:	I		II				IV			bVI	bVII	)
IVd(Δ7):	I		II		III		IV			bVI	bVII	
(Vd:	I		II		III				V		bVII	)
Vd(b9):	I		II		III				V	bVI	bVII	
(Vo:	I	bII			III				V		bVII	)
Vo(b9):	I	bII			III				V	bVI	bVII	
(bVIIo:		bII		bIII		bIV			V		bVII	)
(bVIIo(7):		bII		bIII		bIV			V	bVI	bVII	)
bVIhma:		bII		bIII		bIV			V	bVI	bVII	

	I	II	III / ♭III	III / ♭IV	♭V	V	♯V / ♭VI	♭VII	
(I^{+7}:	**I**		**III**				**♯V**	**♭VII**	**)**
(♭IIImd:	**I**	**♭III**				**V**	**♭VI**	**♭VII**	**)**
♭IIImd(♭9):	**I**	**♭III**		**♭IV**		**V**	**♭VI**	**♭VII**	
Iaug(wt):	**I**	**II**	**III**		**♭V**		**♭VI**	**♭VII**	

pentatonics	hexatonic extensions	generated cnc-scales
(♭IId) ⟶	♭IId(Δ^7) ⟶	♭IImmi
(♭IIId) ⟶	♭IIId(♭9) ⟶	IVmmi
(IVd) ⟶	IVd(Δ^7)	
(Vd) ⟶	Vd(♭9) ⟶	♭VIhma
(Vo) ⟶	Vo(♭9) ⟶	IVhmi
(♭VIIo) ⟶	(♭VIIo(7))	
(♭IIImd) ⟶	♭IIImd(♭9)	
-	-	Iaug(wt)

As under 9) (**Iø^7**), **♭IId(Δ^7)**, **♭IIId(♭9),** and their common extension, the 'altered scale' **♭IImmi**, also show up here. For this reason, **I+^{7}** can be used as an alteration of **I^7**, and **♭IImmi** (or **♭IIId(♭9)**) can be played over it, just like by **Iø^7**.

- If **I** = **G♭**, then **G♭+^{7}** generates the scale **G♭aug(wt),** as well as the 6 hexatonics **Gd(Δ^7), Ad(♭9), Bd(Δ^7), D♭d(♭9), D♭o(♭9),** and **Amd(♭9).** These hexatonics generate the scales **Gmmi (Gd and Ad), Bmmi (Bd and D♭d), Dhma (D♭o and Amd),** and **Bhmi (D♭o).**

Eigenscales

11) IoΔ⁷

IoΔ⁷:	I		♭III			♭V				VII
(Io:	I		♭III		IV	♭V			VI	)
Io(Δ⁷):	I		♭III		IV	♭V			VI	VII
(♯IIo:	I		♯II			♯IV		♯V	VI	)
♯IIo(♯5):	I		♯II			♯IV		♯V	VI	VII
♭Vo:	I		♭III			♭V			VI	VII
(VIo:	I	II	♭III			♭V			VI	)
VIo(9):	I	II	♭III			♭V			VI	VII
(♭VIobl:	I	II			IV			♭VI		VII)
(♭VIobl(7):	I	II			IV	♭V		♭VI		VII)
Idim:	I	II	♭III		IV	♭V		♭VI	VI	VII
(IImd:		II				♯IV	V		VI	VII)
(IImd(♭9):		II	♭III			♯IV	V		VI	VII)
Vhma:	I	II	♭III			♯IV	V		VI	VII
(VIImd:			♯II	III		♯IV		♯V		VII)
VIImd(♭9):	I		♯II	III		♯IV		♯V		VII

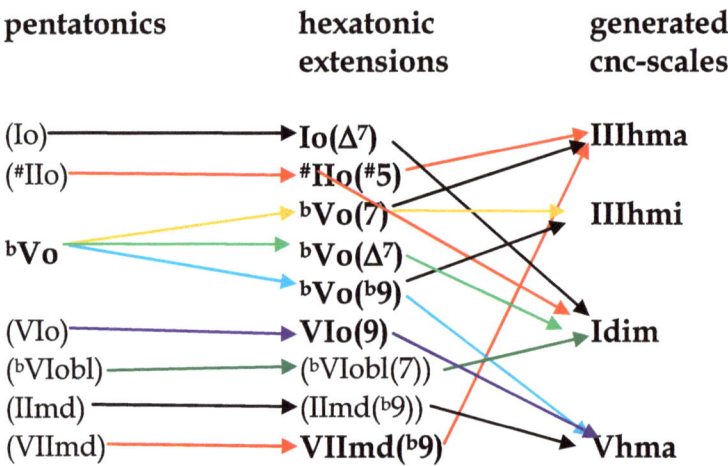

| pentatonics | hexatonic extensions | generated cnc-scales |

Let's consider **I = D♭**. **D♭o∆⁷** generates the pentatonic **Go**, the 3 min-3rd-related hexatonics **D♭o(∆⁷), Eo(♯5), B♭o(9)**, and the hexatonics **E♭md(♭9)** and **Cmd(♭9)**. **Go** generates all the possible scales here, **Fhma/hmi, D♭dim, and A♭hma**.

Eigenscales

12) IøΔ⁷

	I	II	#II	III	#IV	V	VI	VII
IøΔ⁷:	I			III	ᵇV			VII
(VIIp:		II		III	#IV		VI	VII)
VIIp(ᵇ9):	I	II		III	#IV		VI	VII)
(VId:	I	II		III	#IV		VI	)
VId(9):	I	II		III	#IV		VI	VII
(VIId:		II		III	#IV	#V		VII)
VIId(ᵇ9):	I	II		III	#IV	#V		VII
(#IIo:	I		#II		#IV	#V	VI	)
(#IIo(ᵇ9):	I		#II	III	#IV	#V	VI	)
IIIhma:	I		#II	III	#IV	#V	VI	VII
(#IVo:	I		#II		#IV		VI	VII)
#IVo(7):	I		#II	III	#IV		VI	VII
(IImd:		II			#IV	V	VI	VII)
(IImd(9):		II		III	#IV	V	VI	VII)
Vmma:	I	II		III	#IV	V	VI	VII)
(Vmd:	I	II		III		V		VII)
Vmd(Δ⁷):	I	II		III	#IV	V		VII
(VIImd:			#II	III	#IV	#V		VII)
VIImd(ᵇ9):	I		#II	III	#IV	#V		VII)

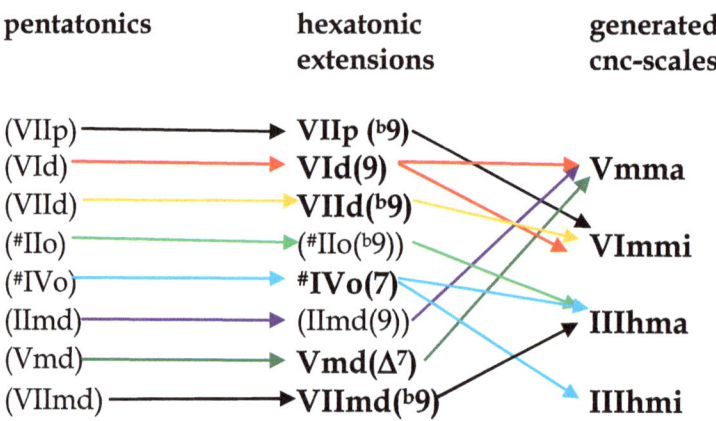

pentatonics	hexatonic extensions	generated cnc-scales

Choosing **I =C**, we find that **CøΔ⁷** generates the 6 hexatonics **Bp/d/md(^{b}9)**, **Ad(9)**, **F#o(7)**, and **Gmd(Δ⁷)**, which in turn generate the scales **Gmma (Ad, Gmd)**, **Ammi (Bp/d, Ad)**, **Ehma (F#o and Bmd)**, and **Ehmi (F#o)**.

Eigenscales

13) I⁴⁷

	I	♭II	II	♭III	III	IV	♭V	V	♭VI	VI	♭VII	
I⁴⁷:	I					IV					♭VII	
Ip:	I			♭III		IV		V			♭VII	
IVp:	I			♭III		IV			♭VI		♭VII	
Vp:	I		II			IV		V			♭VII	
IVd:	I		II			IV			♭VI		♭VII	
(Io:	I			♭III		IV	♭V			VI		)
Io(7):	I			♭III		IV	♭V			VI	♭VII	
(IIIo:		♭II			III			V		VI	♭VII	)
(IIIo(♭9):		♭II			III	IV		V		VI	♭VII	)
IVhma:	I	♭II			III	IV		V		VI	♭VII	
(Vo:	I	♭II			III			V			♭VII	)
Vo(7):	I	♭II			III	IV		V			♭VII	
(VIo:	I		II	♭III			♭V			VI		)
(VIo(♭9):	I		II	♭III			♭V			VI	♭VII	)
♭VIIhma:	I		II	♭III		IV	♭V			VI	♭VII	
(IIIobl:		♭II			III			V	♭VI		♭VII	)
(IIIobl(♭9):		♭II			III	IV		V	♭VI		♭VII	)
IVhmi:	I	♭II			III	IV		V	♭VI		♭VII	
(VIobl:	I	♭II		♭III			♭V			VI		)
(VIobl(♭9):	I	♭II		♭III			♭V			VI	♭VII	)
♭VIIhmi:	I	♭II		♭III		IV	♭V			VI	♭VII	
(Imd:	I				III	IV		V		VI		)
Imd(7):	I				III	IV		V		VI	♭VII	

	I	$\flat$II	II	$\flat$III	IV	$\flat$V	V	$\flat$VI	VI	$\flat$VII	
(I⁴⁷:	**I**				**IV**					$^{\flat}$**VII**	**)**
($^{\flat}$IImd:		$^{\flat}$II			IV	$^{\flat}$V		$^{\flat}$VI		$^{\flat}$VII	)
$^{\flat}$**IImd(Δ⁷):**	**I**	$^{\flat}$**II**			**IV**	$^{\flat}$**V**		$^{\flat}$**VI**		$^{\flat}$**VII**	
($^{\flat}$IIImd:	I			$^{\flat}$III			V	$^{\flat}$VI		$^{\flat}$VII	)
$^{\flat}$**IIImd(9):**	**I**			$^{\flat}$**III**	**IV**		**V**	$^{\flat}$**VI**		$^{\flat}$**VII**	
IVmd:	**I**		**II**		**IV**				**VI**	$^{\flat}$**VII**	
($^{\flat}$VImd:	I	$^{\flat}$II		$^{\flat}$III	IV			$^{\flat}$VI			)
$^{\flat}$**VImd(9):**	**I**	$^{\flat}$**II**		$^{\flat}$**III**	**IV**			$^{\flat}$**VI**		$^{\flat}$**VII**	
($^{\flat}$VIImd:			II	$^{\flat}$III	IV		V			$^{\flat}$VII	)
$^{\flat}$**VIImd(9):**	**I**		**II**	$^{\flat}$**III**	**IV**		**V**			$^{\flat}$**VII**	

Here we have a long list of pentatonics and hexatonics, due to the fact that the chord consists of only 3 notes.

pentatonics	hexatonic extensions	generated cnc-scales	hexatonic extensions	pentatonics

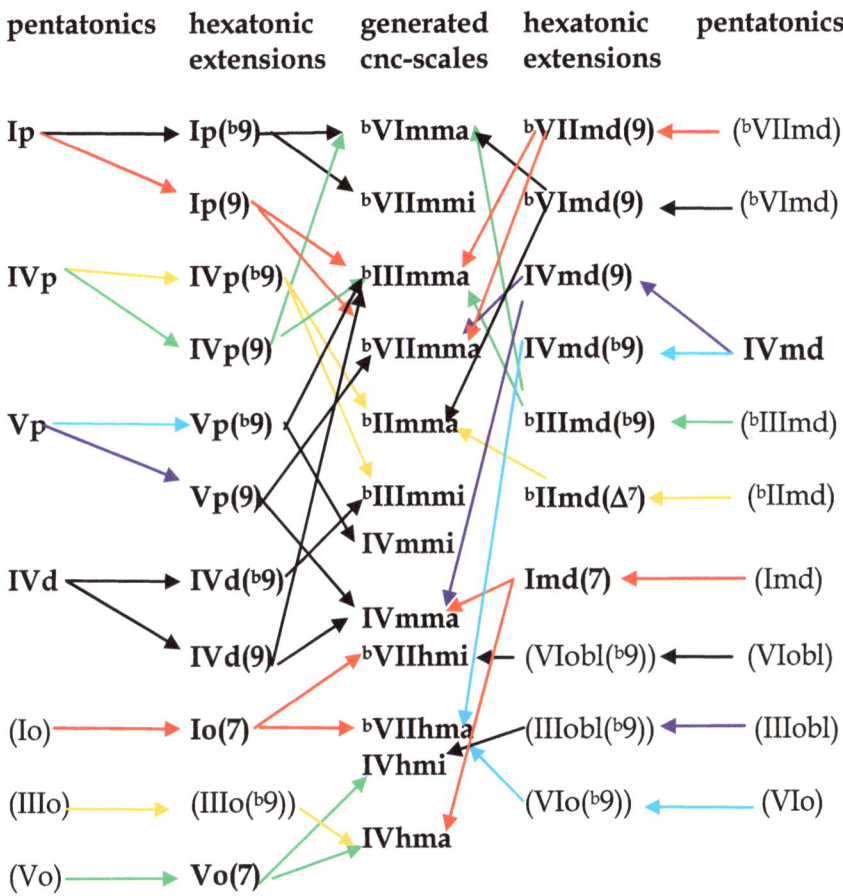

Let **I = Eᵇ**, **Eᵇ⁴⁷** generates the pentatonics **Eᵇp, Bᵇp, Aᵇp/d/md,** as well as the hexatonics **Eᵇo(7), Bᵇo(7), Eᵇmd(7), Emd(Δ⁷), Gᵇmd(9), Bmd(9),** and **Dᵇmd(9);** which in turn generate the scales **Gᵇmma, Bmma, Dᵇmma, Dᵇmmi, Emma, Gᵇmmi, Aᵇmma, Aᵇmmi, Dᵇhma, Dᵇhmi, Aᵇhma,** and **Aᵇhmi.**

As we see, the chord **X⁴⁷** offers a vast amount of interpretable possibilities. **5 pentatonics** and **7 hexatonics**, which extend to **5 mma-scales, 3 mmi-scales, 2 hma-scales,** and **2 hmi-scales** that can be used with this chord! In this case, unlike in others, you can really make use of the entire scale without coming across any 'non-harmonic notes'. This feature makes the chord very interesting for the ambitious improviser. For example, consider a piece like Herbie Hancock's 'Maiden Voyage', constructed exclusively from X^{47}-chords. It can be a real voyage through several parallel universes for you and your improvisational spaceship.

Coming back to earth from these spacy considerations in order to get a handy formula to keep all of these scales you can use in mind, observe that the roots of the **5 mma-scales** that belong to E^{b47} form the pentatonic $D^b p$ (D^b, E, G^b, A^b, B). The roots of the **3 mmi-scales** are just the I, IV, and V of this same pentatonic (D^b, G^b, A^b), while the roots of the **2 hma/hmi-scales** are the I and V of $D^b p$.

Generally, we can state this rule, which is not too hard to remember :

Over I^{47}, we can make use of the **mma-scales** with their roots inside ^{b}**VIIp;**

the **mmi-scales** with the roots **I′, IV′,** and **V′** of that pentatonic (^{b}VII, ^{b}III, and IV); and the **hma/hmi-scales** with roots **I′** and **V′** (^{b}VII and IV).

For another example, let's use the rule on B^{b47}. It tells us that we can use the **mma-scales** with the roots A^b, B, D^b, $E^{b\prime}$, and G^b; the **mmi-scales** with the roots A^b, D^b, and E^b; as well as the **hma/hmi-scales** with the roots A^b and D^b.

14) I⁴Δ⁷

I⁴Δ⁷:	I			IV					VII
(Id:	I	ᵇIII		IV		V		IV	)
Id(Δ⁷):	I	ᵇIII		IV		V		IV	VII
(IId:		II		IV		V		VI	VII)
IId(7):	I	II		IV		V		VI	VII)
(Io:	I	ᵇIII		IV	ᵇV			VI	)
Io(Δ⁷)*:	I	ᵇIII		IV	ᵇV			VI	VII
(VIIo:		II	III	IV			ᵇVI		VII)
VIIo(ᵇ9):		II	III	IV			ᵇVI		VII
ᵇVIobl**:	I	II		IV			ᵇVI		VII)
(Imd:	I		III	IV		V		VI	)
Imd(Δ⁷):	I		III	IV		V		VI	VII
(Vmd:	I	II	III			V			VII)
Vmd(7):	I	II	III	IV		V			VII

*Of the min-3ʳᵈ-relatives of Io, the hexatonics **ᵇIIIo(9)** and **ᵇVo(Δ⁷)** could also belong to the list.

Of the min-3ʳᵈ-relatives of **ᵇVIobl, the hexatonics **IIobl(7)**, **IVobl(5)**, and *Of the min-3ʳᵈ-relatives of Io, the hexatonics **ᵇIIIo(9)** and **ᵇVo(Δ⁷)** could also belong to the list.

| pentatonics | hexatonic extensions | generated cnc-scales |

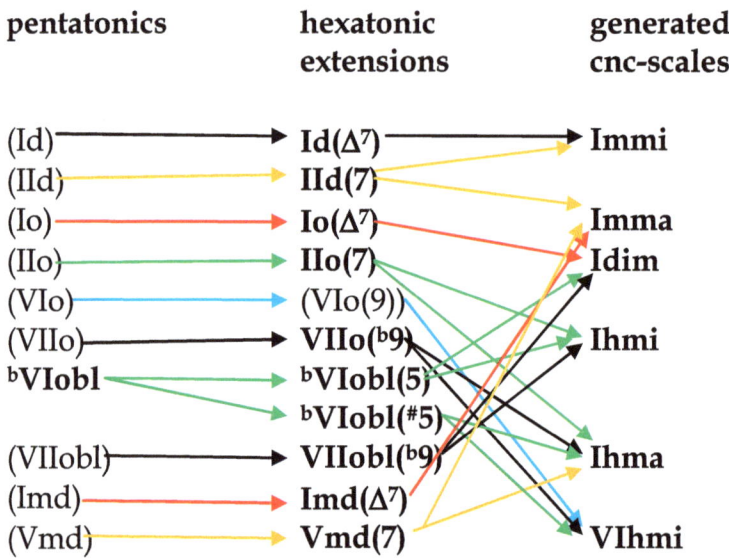

As an example, we choose **I = F. F⁴Δ⁷** generates the pentatonic **Dᵇobl** and the 9 additional hexatonics **Fd(Δ⁷), Gd(7), Fo(Δ⁷), Go(7), Do(9), Eo(ᵇ9), Eobl(ᵇ9), Fmd(Δ⁷), and Cmd(7);** these hexatonics generate the 6 scales **Fmma/mmi/hma/hmi, Fdim, and Dhmi.**

Finally, I would like to comprise our main results in a concluding list:

chords	pentatonics	additional hexatonics	generated scales
1) Io	I/ᵇIII/ᵇV/VIo, I/ᵇIII/ᵇV/VIobl	-	ᵇII/III/V/ᵇVII-hmi/a, I/ᵇIIdim
2) Io⁷	ᵇIIId, ᵇVobl	Io(7), VIo(ᵇ9)	ᵇIImma/i, ᵇIIImmi, Vhmi, ᵇVIIhmi/a, ᵇIIdim
3) I-⁷	Ip, ᵇIIImd	ᵇIIIobl(5), ᵇVIIo(9)	ᵇIII/ᵇVImma, ᵇVIImma/i, Vhmi, ᵇVIhma, ᵇIIdim
4) I-Δ⁷	-	Id(Δ⁷), #IVo(ᵇ9)	Imm/hmi, IIIhmi, Vhma, Iaug(hta)
5) I⁷	Vd, Vo	Imd(7), ᵇIIo(Δ⁷), ᵇIIImd(9), IIIo(#5), ᵇVIIo(9)	IVmma/i, Vmmi, IVhmi/a, ᵇVIhma, ᵇVIIdim, (VIIdim)

chords	pentatonics	additional hexatonics	generated scales
6) IΔ^7	Vmd	Imd(Δ^7)	I/Vmma, IIIhmi, Ihma, Iaug(hta)
7) I+Δ^7	-	Vmd($^\flat$9), VIId/o/md($^\flat$9)	VImm/hmi, I/IIIhma, Iaug(hta)
9)* I$\emptyset^7$	-	Iobl(7), $^\flat$IId/o(Δ^7), $^\flat$III/VId($^\flat$9), Vd(Δ^7)	$^\flat$II/Vmmi, $^\flat$IIdim, Iaug(wt)
10) I+^{7}	-	$^\flat$II/IVd (Δ^7), $^\flat$IIId/md ($^\flat$9), Vd/o ($^\flat$9)	$^\flat$IImmi, IVmm/hmi, $^\flat$VIhma, Iaug(wt)
11) IoΔ^7	$^\flat$Vo	Io(Δ^7), $^\sharp$IIo($^\sharp$5), VIo(9), VIImd($^\flat$9)	IIIhmi/a, Vhma, Idim
12) I$\emptyset\Delta^7$	-	$^\sharp$IVo(7), Vmd (Δ^7), , VId(9), VIIp/d/md ($^\flat$9)	Vmma, VImmi, IIIhmi/a

*Remember that we did not include 8) I+ in our list.

Eigenscales

chords	pentatonics	add. hexatonics	generated scales
13) I^{47}	I/IV/Vp, IVd/md	Io/md(7), ♭IImd(Δ^7), ♭III/♭VI/♭VIImd(9), IIIo (♭9), Vo(7)	♭II/♭VImma, ♭II/IV/♭VIImma/I, IV ♭VIIhmi/a
14) $I^4\Delta^7$	♭VIobl	Id/o/md (Δ^7), IId/o(7), Vmd(7), VIIo/obl (♭9)	Imma/i, Ihmi/a, VIhmi, Idim

Remarks:

Chords 1-7, the most traditional ones, all belong either to ♭IIdim (1-3, 5) or to Iaug(hta) (4, 6, 7). The only chords that neither belong to a dim or an aug scale are 11) I∅Δ^7 and 13) I^{47}.

The Special Role of the Dominant 7th Chord

The Use of 'Altered Scales'

In improvisational practice over the years, it has become clear that the chord I^7 is very open in that it allows the use of many different 'altered scales' (for the expression 'altered notes', see p. 67). I would like to consider this fact in the light of the pentatonic approach.

Generally, the 3rd and the 7th of the tetrachords of chap. 3 with a perf 5th as a 3rd note (chords 3, 4, 5, and 6) can be considered to be their most characteristic notes. You may leave out the 5th, which we called 'the small octave' in chap. 3, in the chord voicing and the chords will still have their characteristic sound (try it out!). One of these chords is the 'Dominant 7th' (chord 5 of chap. 3).

Observe that this chord, in the form V^7, is simultaneously the 5th degree of all 4 types of 7-note-cnc-scales, **Imma/i/hmi/a** (see p. 35 ff). It is not difficult to verify that it is the only chord type to appear in all these scales at the same place. Maybe this feature of the Dominant 7th is exactly what makes it singular among the 12 tetrachord qualities (we do not consider the triads 13), 14) here).

In practice, often chord voicings are used that leave out the 5th. Anyway, an accompanist should limit himself to the necessary, in order to give the soloist the most possible freedom. This freedom includes the free choice of scales that contain the ♭5 or #5 of the Dominant 7th, or both.

The goal of this chapter is to provide a list of all of the eigenscales containing the 3 characteristic chord notes **1**, **3**, and **7**, of I^7. This amounts to summing up everything we have covered in the previous chapter under 5) (I^7), 9) ($I\varnothing^7$), and 10) ($I+^7$) ($I\varnothing^7$ containing ♭5, $I+^7$ containing #5, instead of 5). - There is even one hexatonic that contains neither 5, ♭5, nor #5, **IVmd(Δ^7)**, but we will not include it in our list as its root is the 'problematic' **4th** of our chord.

Gathering scales for our list, we take the freedom to interpret any Dominant 7th chord not only in its traditional role that gave the chord its name (the **5th** degree of a **mma/i/hmi/a-scale**), but also possibly the **3rd** degree of a **hma-scale**, the **4th** or **7th** degree of a **mmi-scale**, the **2nd**, **4th**, **#5th**, or **7th degree of** a **dim scale**, or any degree of an **aug(wt)-scale**; because these are all places where a $I^7(\backslash 5^{th})$ chord can show up.

- And here comes the impressive list:

The Special Role of the Dominant 7th Chord

chord	pentatonics	additional hexatonics	generated cnc-scales
$I^7(\backslash5)$	Vd, Vo	Iobl/md(7), ^{b}IId/o(Δ^7), ^{b}IIId/md(^{b}9), IIIo($^\#$5), VId(^{b}9), ^{b}VIIo(9)	^{b}II/Vmmi, ^{b}VIhma, ^{b}VIIdim, (VIIdim), Iaug(wt)

Counting the scales, we have 2 pentatonics, 9 additional hexatonics, and 6 cnc- scales which you can use if you stumble over a Dominant 7th chord (and an accompanist who leaves you space by using open chord voicings).

There are 2 extended, 'altered', Dominant 7th chords with a special sound that are often used in Jazz and Blues tunes: I^{7b9} and $I^{7\#9}$. As their names tell us, they are the Dominant 7th chord with the ^{b}9 and $^\#$9 added, respectively. Consequently, they are pentachords. Leaving out the 5th, they become tetrachords, and that is how I would like to define them:

I^{7b9}:	I	^{b}II		III		^{b}VII

$I^{7\#9}$:	I		$^\#$II	III		^{b}VII

The most common voicing of $I^{7\#9}$ is I - III - ^{b}VII - $^\#$II', giving #II the highest pitch ($E^{7\#9}$: E - G$^\#$ - B - D'). On the other hand, the most common voicing of I^{7b9}, ^{b}II - III - V - ^{b}VII, employs the 5th. This is also the tetrachord ^{b}IIo. So, the pentachord I^{7b9}, I - ^{b}II - III - V - ^{b}VII, can be interpreted as the tetrachord ^{b}IIo, with root I added.

This latter chord is very commonly defined as the Dominant 7th of the minor II-V-I-progression (see chap. 10, p. 105).

Though the 2 chords have mostly different eigenscales, a close examination shows that all the eigenscales of one of them can be used with the other as well. In all eigenscales of I^{7b9} you can insert #9 without contradicting rule 2 of chap. 3, and vice versa. Thus the following list contains the eigenscales of both chords without distinction:

The Special Role of the Dominant 7th Chord

list of eigenscales of $I^{7\flat9}$ and $I^{7\sharp9}$

pentatonics	hexatonic extensions	generated cnc-scales
Vo	Iobl(7), ♭IId/o(Δ7), ♭IIId/md(♭9), IIIo(#5), ♭VIIo(9)	♭IImmi, ♭VIhma, ♭VIIdim, (VIIdim)

I added the 'Coltrane scale' **VIIdim** containing the ♭9, as it fits $I^{7\flat9}$ well and is a good interpretation of $I^{7\sharp9}$, as your ear will tell you.

Comparing this list with the former (of $I^7(\backslash 5)$), you will find that it is completely contained within it. In this respect, you can consider this last list to contain all of the scales you can use on any of the **'altered'** **Dominant 7th chords** $I^{\varnothing 7}$, I^{+7}, $I^{7\flat9}$, and $I^{7\sharp9}$.

However, even this list is not yet exhaustive. There is still the phenomenon of the 'blue note' ♭III that can be used on the chord I^7 (which can be interpreted as the #9 of the chord). If we look up all scales that contain this note and simultaneously do NOT contain the (problematic) notes IV and VII, then we get these additional scales (which do not necessarily contain all chord notes):

I^7/5:	I				III					♭VII
#IIp:		#I		#II		#IV		#V	#VI	
#IIp(♭9):		#I		#II	III	#IV		#V	#VI	
VIp(#11):	I		(II)	#II	III		V		VI	
#IIo:	#VII			#II		#IV		#V	VI	
#IIo(7):	#VII	#I		#II		#IV		#V	VI	
#Ihmi:	#VII	#I		#II	III	#IV		#V	VI	
#IIo(Δ7):	#VII		II	#II		#IV		#V	VI	
#IIobl:	I			#II		#IV	V		VI	
#IIobl(5):	I			♭III		#IV	V		VI	♭VII
♭Vobl:	I			♭III		♭V			VI	♭VII
Vhmi:	I		II	♭III		#IV	V		VI	♭VII
VIo:	I		II	♭III		♭V			VI	
VIo(♭9):	I		II	♭III		♭V			VI	♭VII

The Special Role of the Dominant 7th Chord

(I⁷/5:	I			III			ᵇVII)
VIobl:	I	ᵇII	ᵇIII		ᵇV	VI	

Let's take a closer look at the scale **VIp(#11)**. It is obviously much the same as the usual **VI-Blues-Pentatonic,** in which traditionally the #11 is often added. I put the 11 (II) in brackets, because according to our definitions, **VIp(#11)** is not a genuine scale (containing 2 consecutive h.s.). The use of exactly the other 5 notes creates phrases similar to or identical with often heard and used Blues phrases. Another way to produce similar results is to think in terms of **Id(3)**:

Id(3):	I		#II	III	(IV)		V	VI

VIp(#11):	I	(II)	#II	III			V	VI

Comparing **VIp(#11)** and **Id(3)**, we see that they are the same, except for the notes in brackets. I put the IV in brackets as Id(3) is not a genuine scale, either. The use of the IV does make sense though, but only when used in a 'non-linear' fashion and not in simple ascending or descending lines. You would start for example with I, jump to IV (a 'problematic' note, by the way!), back to #II, then on to III… Try it out, and decide for yourself in which way you prefer to 'think' of this scale, as **VIp(#11)** or rather as **Id(3)**!

'Horizontal' Playing

'Horizontal' playing is a term used by George Russell in his influential book 'The Lydian Chromatic Concept Of Tonal Organization In Improvisation'. It means, more or less, that you take a look at the signs at the beginning of a tune and use the melodic major scale that corresponds with these signs in improvisation. For example, four b-signs suggest the use of A♭mma. Here, the term 'horizontal' might be explained by this picture: compare improvisation to a walk through a city. The houses you encounter on your way are the chords of a chord progression. Improvising horizontally then means you walk just straight (horizontally) along the streets, instead of entering the houses on your way and walking up stairs, in order to explore what is inside them; which would correspond to improvising 'vertically', or to let your choice of notes be influenced by the single chords.

Note: George Russell himself suggested the mixed use of horizontal and vertical playing. The starting point of his theory was in fact that he wasn't quite satisfied with the sound of the Imma-scale played on the chord I∆7. We already talked about the scale note **IV** not sounding 'good' in this context. Indeed, later on some theorists even called **IV** a 'diatonic non-harmonic note' (the **Xmma**-scales, as well as the notes belonging to them, are sometimes called 'diatonic').

Russell suggested to substitute the **IV** with **#IV**. The **#IV** does sound better indeed, but using it, you actually find yourself in another scale, **Vmma:**

Imma (with raised 4th):	I	II	III	#IV	V	VI	VII	I
	↕	↕	↕	↕	↕	↕	↕	↕
Renumeration (V = I′):	IV′	V′	VI′	VII′	I′	II′	III′	IV′

(I′mma = Vmma)

That is, you interpret I∆7 as **IV′**∆7, the 4th degree of **Vmma.**

This is definitely a possible solution.

Note that **Vmma** is identical with the scale **'I Lydian'**. Hence the expression 'Lydian' in the title of Russell's book.

Let us compare the solution that our pentatonic approach suggests, the pentatonic **Vmd** (see 6), p. 112):

Vmd: **I   II   III   V   VII**

As you see, there is a gap between III and V; neither IV nor #IV is used. Thus, in a way, we do not actually decide if we are moving in **Imma** or in **Vmma** (note that **Vmd** is embedded in both scales).

This is a good example of what I said in the very beginning. In my opinion, complete scales are just too big for the use in many improvisational situations. Pentatonic improvisation is, in fact, a 'less is more' approach. We basically use 5 notes instead of 7, and occasionally add more notes not necessarily contained in the mma-scale in question (like, f.i., ♭III in the case of **Vmd**).

The horizontal approach is the most simple improvisation strategy, you use the same notes throughout the whole tune. Therefore, we start our practical considerations with it. However, we modify it by using a pentatonic instead of a melodic major scale

.

Turnarounds

We start with a progression of 4 chords which are all part of the same Imma-scale, are frequently found in many branches of popular music, and also form part of several jazz standards. The 'turnaround':

$$\mathbf{I\Delta^7 - VI^{-7} - II^{-7} - V^7}$$

The label 'turnaround' stresses the fact that $\mathbf{V^7}$ leads back to $\mathbf{I\Delta^7}$ in quite a natural way, enabling one to go on with this progression in a circular fashion, infinitely. In fact, you can find loads of tunes which just consist of these 4 chords.

As an example, we choose **I** to be **B♭** and thus have the progression:

$$\mathbf{B^\flat\Delta^7 - G^{-7} - C^{-7} - F^7}.$$

The chords all belong to **B♭mma**, so the horizontal approach would mean to use this scale throughout the progression. I suggest to use the 'parallel Blues pentatonic', **Gp** with the additional 'Blue Note' **D♭**, instead:

$$ G - B♭ - (C) - D♭ - D - F, $$

This is **VIp(#11)** of the last chapter, with **I = B♭**. There, it was used to interpret the Dominant 7th chord **I⁷**, but it is a valid interpretation of **IΔ⁷** as well, containing neither the 7 nor the Δ⁷ of the chord.

Let us now see in detail how our pentatonic scale corresponds to the chords of the progression. To make this easier to follow, I will write down the chords together with the pentatonic scale, indicating which chord notes and chord extensions the pentatonic contains.

$$ \begin{array}{ccccccc} & 13 & 1 & 9 & ♭3 & 3 & 5 \\ \textbf{B♭Δ⁷:} & \textbf{G} - & \textbf{B♭} - & \textbf{(C)} - & \textbf{D♭} - & \textbf{D} - & \textbf{F} \end{array} $$

The pentatonic contains the chord's maj and min 3rd simultaneously. This fact is responsible for the bluesy colour of the improvisation.

$$ \begin{array}{ccccccc} & 1 & ♭3 & 11 & \#11 & 5 & 7 \\ \textbf{G-⁷:} & \textbf{G} - & \textbf{Bb} - & \textbf{(C)} - & \textbf{Db} - & \textbf{D} - & \textbf{F} \end{array} $$

$$ \begin{array}{ccccccc} & 5 & 7 & 1 & ♭9 & 9 & 11 \\ \textbf{C-⁷:} & \textbf{G} - & \textbf{Bb} - & \textbf{(C)} - & \textbf{Db} - & \textbf{D} - & \textbf{F} \end{array} $$

$$ \begin{array}{ccccccc} & 9 & 11 & 5 & \#5 & 13 & 1 \\ \textbf{F⁷:} & \textbf{G} - & \textbf{Bb} - & \textbf{(C)} - & \textbf{Db} - & \textbf{D} - & \textbf{F} \end{array} $$

You see, the 'non-diatonic' note **D♭** adds an interesting flavour to the rest of the chords. It is the **#11** of **G-⁷**, the **♭9** of **C-⁷** (altering with the chord's 9), and the **#5** of **F⁷**, an altered note. The note in parentheses, **C**, is comparably less interesting, at least on the last 2 chords. It is the root of **C-⁷**, and the 5th of **F⁷**. -

Generally, I would like to state as **a rough rule**:

Improvising horizontally means: find out to which Imma-scale the chords in question belong, then use the parallel Blues pentatonic VIp throughout the progression; or, more specifically, use the scale:

VI   I   (II) #II III   V VI

Alternatively, you can use the very similar **Id(3)** (see p. 90).

Often the turnaround is used as a rapid half-bar progression

| IΔ7 VI-7 | II-7 V7 |

which makes the horizontal approach a reasonable choice.

However, please keep in mind that the rule is a rough one, and accordingly the approximation of the chord progression by the pentatonic scale is also a rough one. This especially holds true for the Dominant 7th chord **V**[7] (**F**[7] in the example above), as the pentatonic contains the problematic **11**[th] of the chord (**B**[b] in our example).

Major II-V-I Chord Progressions

These chord progressions are very frequently found in jazz standards. Their exact form is:

$$\text{II-}^7 \ - \ \text{V}^7 - \text{I}\Delta^7.$$

Studying the list of scales at the end of chap. 6, we find loads of possibilities for improvising on these 3 chords. However, I would like to discuss only the most common interpretations here.

Our strategy to improvise over them, in short, is:

1) Start with the pentatonic **IIp** on **II-⁷**.

2) When the progression switches to **V⁷**, alter one or more notes of **IIp** in order to obtain one of these new scales:

a) **IId** – b) **IIo** – c) **IVo(7)** – d) **ᵇVImmi** – e) **VIIo(7)** – f) **IIdim –g) bIIIdim***

3) When **IΔ⁷** comes along, 'dissolve' into the pentatonic **Vmd** or alternatively, as it is in most cases easier to think of, **IΔ⁷⁹** (the 2 scales are equal, see p. 42; there: **Imd = IVΔ⁷⁹**).

The term 'dissolution' stems from classical times and describes a feeling of tension and subsequent relaxation when you listen to these kinds of chord progressions. The arousal of this feeling can be attributed to the fact that the presence of a **tritone** in a scale (all of the scales under 2) contain one or more) produces a feeling of tension which is dissolved (vanishes) when the next scale, **Vmd** (a scale that does NOT contain any tritones), is played over **IΔ⁷**.

It turns out that, using this strategy, we make use of more and more

---

* Transforming **V** to **I'**, we get **I'⁷** instead of **V⁷**, and these scales become a) **V'd** – b) **V'o** – c) **ᵇVII'o(7)** – d) **ᵇII'mmi** – e) **III'o(7)** – f) **ᵇVII'dim** – g) **VII'dim** (actually **V'dim** and **ᵇVI'dim**). The pentatonics (a, b) and the diminished scales (f, g) are exactly those in the list at the end of chap. 6, under 5) **I⁷** (p. 75). The hexatonic extensions (c, e) are a little different than those in the list, it has **ᵇVII'o(9)** and **III'o(#5)** instead, as those hexatonic extensions contain the whole chord. **ᵇII'mmi**, the altered scale of **I⁷**, is not contained in the list, as it rather belongs to one of the altered chords **Iø⁷** or **I+⁷** (see 9) and 10) of the list on p. 82).

altered notes proceeding from a) to g) in the **II-V**-part of the progression.

Now, let's examine this strategy in detail. As an example, we choose the concrete progression **G-7 - C7 - FΔ7**.

a) the simplest strategy is to choose the 'scale progression'

$$\text{Gp - Gd - FΔ}^{79} \quad \text{(or, generally, IIp – IId - IΔ}^{79}\text{)}.$$

It looks like this:

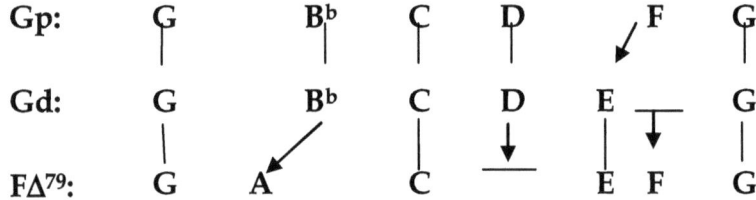

To go from **Gp** to **Gd** means no more than just to 'flatten' **F** into **E**. To dissolve from there to **FΔ79** means to flatten **Bb** into **A**, drop **D**, and re-insert **F**. Note that since **Gp = G-7/11**, and **Gd = C79**, our strategy amounts to playing the 'extended chord progression' **G-7/11 - C79 - FΔ79**.

b) the first alternative is to play the scale progression

$$\text{Gp - Go - FΔ}^{79} \quad \text{(IIp – IIo - IΔ}^{79}\text{)}:$$

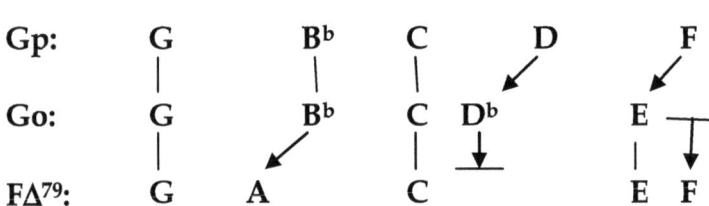

To go from **Gp** to **Go** means to flatten 2 notes, **D** into **Db**, and **F** into **E**. The dissolution to **FΔ79** is quite similar as before, only we drop **Db** instead of **D**.

The corresponding extended chord progression here is

G-7/11 - C7b9 - FΔ79. **C7b9** is often called an 'alteration' of **C7**, as it contains the 'altered' note ♭9 (see p. 67). Our different strategies amount to using different alterations of **C⁷**, as we will see.

Note: using the hexatonic **Go(7)** instead of **Go** simplifies the matter and sounds alright. However, doing so means to keep **F** throughout the changes; although it is a 'problematic note' over **C⁷**.

c) Next, instead of using **Go**, we **step up a min 3ʳᵈ** and choose **B♭o(7)**. Thus, here the scale progression is:

$$\textbf{Gp - B♭o(7) - F}\Delta^{79} \qquad \textbf{(IIp – IVo(7) - I}\Delta^{79}\textbf{)}:$$

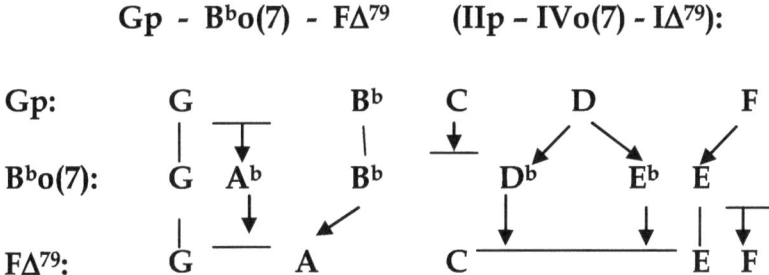

Here, to go from **Gp** to **B♭o(7)** amounts to changing quite a lot. We need to flatten **F** as before, 'split' **D** into **D♭** and **E♭**, to drop **C**, and insert **A♭** (the dropping of C is optional, as the root of **C⁷** it could of course be kept). Do not let yourself get discouraged. The task is not to learn which notes to keep and which to change, the task is to learn all of the different scales by heart and then to practice the changes from one into another. Which does of course amount to doing some work.

The new notes in **B♭o(7)**, **A♭** and **E♭**, are the altered notes #5 and #9 of C⁷, respectively. As the unaltered 5ᵗʰ, **G**, is also contained in this scale, we call the #5 ♭13 here, for the sake of clarity. The use of #9 (= ♭3) adds a blues-like flavor to your improvisation, as the 3 (E) is also there.

The corresponding extended chord progression would be **G-⁷/¹¹ - C⁷♭9#9♭13 - F**Δ⁷⁹.

d) Now, **we move on another min 3rd** from **B♭** to **D♭**, and our next scale progression becomes:

$$\textbf{Gp - D♭mmi - F}\Delta^{79} \qquad \textbf{(IIp – ♭VImmi - I}\Delta^{79}\textbf{)}:$$

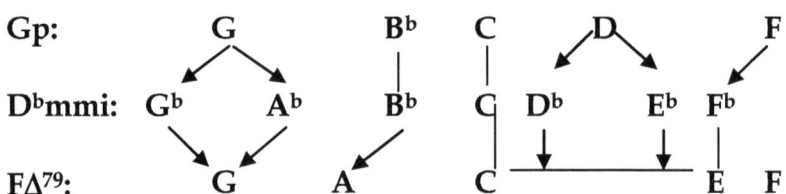

Here, the transition from **Gp** to **D♭mmi** can be achieved by a double splitting of **G** into **G♭** and **A♭**, and of **D** into **D♭** and **E♭**, plus the flattening of **F** into **F♭**.

D♭mmi is often called the 'altered scale' of **C⁷** and contains all possible altered notes of **C⁷** (compare p. 67).

In this case, it might seem simpler to think in terms of **Cmd** rather than **FΔ⁷⁹**; as in the corresponding scale progression **Gp** – **D♭mmi** – **Cmd** the 'root progression' **D♭** - **C** is a h.s., instead of the maj 3rd **D♭** - **F**. On the other hand, the parallels between the **maj** and **min II-V-I-progressions** (see p. 106) suggest sticking to

$$\text{Gp} - \text{D}^\flat\text{mmi} - \text{F}\Delta^{79}.$$

Note that under a), we could have completed **Gd** to obtain **Gmmi**, an eigenscale of **C⁷** (p. 81, 5)). As it does not contain **F**, the 'problematic' 11 of **G⁷**, we are free to use this scale in improvisation instead of **Gd**. That is to say, we generally have the choice of 2 alternative mmi-scales to play in maj II-V-I situations, **IImmi** and **♭VImmi,** their roots being a tritone apart. These are two eigenscales of **Vø⁷**, one of the altered Dominant 7th chords (with **V = I'**, we get **II = V'** and **♭VI = ♭II'** and thus **IImmi = =V'mmi** and **♭VImmi = ♭II'mmi,** two eigenscales of **Iø'⁷**; see p. 68).

In this situation, when the improviser uses one of these two scales, the accompanist is also free to play **♭II⁷** instead of **V⁷.**; that is, to play the altered chord progression **II-⁷ - ♭II⁷ – I.** Actually, it would be more exact to say that we first substitute **V⁷** with **Vø⁷** and then switch freely to **♭IIø'⁷,** which has the same eigenscales as **Vø⁷** (see p. 68; there: **Iø⁷ = ♭Vø⁷**)). This chord substitution has been called 'tritone substitution', and since the bebop days accompanists (and also composers) have felt free to make use of this substitution (one example is 'The Girl From Ipanema', see p. 140). The corresponding extended chord progression is **G-⁷/¹¹ – C alt - FΔ⁷⁹**, if

Major II-V-I Chord Progressions

we agree to call **C alt** the chord **C⁷** containing all possible altered notes, **♭5/#5**, and **♭9/#9**.

e) To **complete the circle of minor 3rds, we go on again a min 3ʳᵈ** from **D♭** to **E**, and the corresponding scale progression is:

$$\text{Gp - Eo(7) - F}\Delta^{79} \qquad \text{(IIp – VIIo(7) - I}\Delta^{79}\text{):}$$

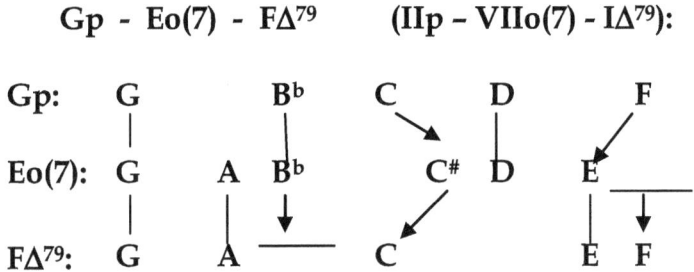

Corresponding extended chord progression: **G⁻⁷ᐟ¹¹ – C⁷ᐟ♭⁹ᐟ⁹ᐟ¹³ - F∆⁷⁹**.

f) The next scale progression to examine is

$$\text{Gp - Gdim - F}\Delta^{79} \qquad \text{(IIp – IIdim - I}\Delta^{79}\text{):}$$

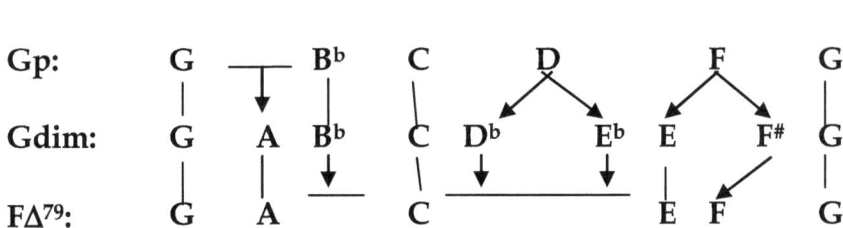

Gdim contains the 4 chord notes **C, E, G,** and **B♭**, the chord extension **13**, **A,** of **C⁷**, and the 3 altered notes **♭9, #9,** and **♭5**.

g) The last possibility I would like to discuss is the use of still another diminished scale, namely **A♭dim,** a h.s. higher. This yields:

Gp - A^bdim - FΔ⁷⁹   **(IIp – ^bIIIdim - IΔ⁷⁹):**

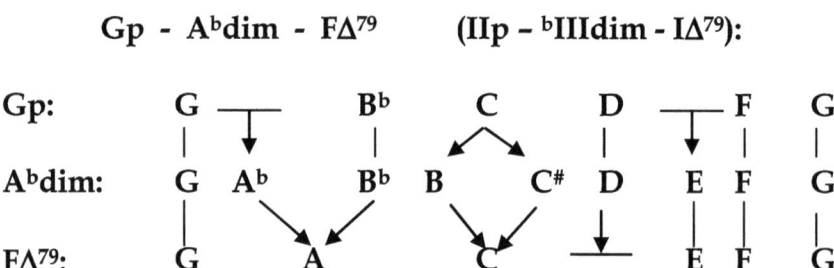

A^bdim contains the chord notes **3, 5,** and **7,** of **C⁷,** the chord extensions **9** and (the usually problematic) **11,** the altered note **#5,** the **7 (B^b),** and peculiarly also the **Δ⁷ (B)**; the latter coming in by way of the double splitting of **C** into **B** and **C#.** Strangely enough, this progression of notes works well with the chord (try it out!). John Coltrane made extensive use of it, as I already mentioned in chap. 6 (p. 60).

Note: In up-tempo-tunes, as well as in the case of half-bar-progressions

$$|\,II\text{-}^{7}\,V^{7}\,|\,I\Delta^{7}\,|$$

we can use simplified scale progressions. The rule is to leave out the first scale, **Gp,** and play one of the second scales over both **II-⁷** and **V⁷.** This amounts to playing altered notes already over **II-⁷** and doesn't arouse any problems.

Summary: For improvising on a **maj II-V-I** progression, I use one of these corresponding scale progressions:

a) IIp - IId - IΔ⁷⁹;

alternatively,

IIp - IImmi - IΔ⁷⁹

b) IIp - IIo(7) - IΔ⁷⁹

c) IIp - IVo(7) - IΔ⁷⁹

Major II-V-I Chord Progressions

d) IIp - ^{b}VImmi - IΔ^{79}

or, equivalently,

IIp - ^{b}VImmi - Vmd

e) IIp - VIIo(7) - IΔ^{79}

f) IIp - IIdim - IΔ^{79}

g) IIp - ^{b}IIIdim - IΔ^{79}

In up-tempo-tunes und half-bar progressions, the scale progressions shorten to:

a) IId - IΔ^{79} (IImmi - IΔ^{79})

b) IIo(7) - IΔ^{79}

c) IVo(7) - IΔ^{79}

d) ^{b}VImmi - IΔ^{79} (^{b}VImmi - Vmd)

e) VIIo(7) - IΔ^{79}

f) IIdim - IΔ^{79}

g) ^{b}IIIdim - IΔ^{79}

Minor II-V-I Chord Progressions

A minor II - V - I chord progression can also be very frequently found in jazz standards. It has the form:

$$\text{IIo}^7 - \text{V}^7 - \text{I-}\Delta^7.$$

This is its purest form, in the sense that all 3 chords (IIo^7, V^7, and $\text{I-}\Delta^7$) belong to the same scale, **Ihmi.** In concrete standards, the last chord ($\text{I-}\Delta^7$) is often replaced by I-^7, I-^6, or simply the minor triad **I-**. However, regardless of which chord we find in a given situation, the scales we are going to use in our improvisation remain the same, as we will see in a moment.

The dominant 7th chord here is usually given as $\text{V}^{7\flat9}$. The $\flat9$ of V^7 is contained in **Ihmi**, thus $\text{V}^{7\flat9}$ is also an eigenchord of the scale.

The situation here is even a bit simpler than in the major case:

a) Over the first 2 chords of the progression, IIo^7 and $\text{V}^{7(\flat9)}$, we can use the same pentatonic, namely IIo(7). The reason is that it contains all the chord notes of those 2 chords*:

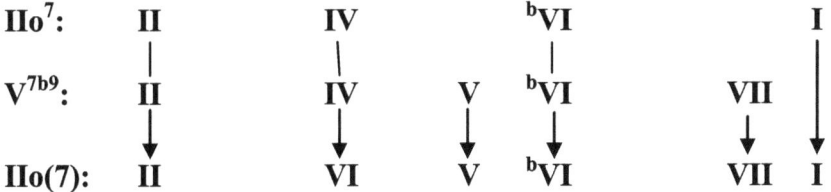

Then, on the last chord, we dissolve to **Id.** (As to the term 'dissolution', see p. 95.) This latter pentatonic always fits well, be it I-^7, **I-**, $\text{I-}\Delta^7$, or I-^6. The following diagram shows why.

---

*The results of chap. 6 also show that IIo(7) is an eigenscale of both IIo^7 and V^7. Indeed, if we make the transitions $\text{II} = \text{I}'$ and $\text{V} = \text{I}''$, then we have $\text{IIo(7)} = \text{I}'\text{o(7)} = \text{V}''\text{o(7)}$, $\text{IIo}^7 = \text{I}'\text{o}^7$, and $\text{V}^7 = \text{I}''^7$. Our statement becomes: $\text{I}'\text{o(7)} = \text{V}''\text{o(7)}$ is an eigenscale of both $\text{I}'\text{o}^7$ and I''^7. This example can be found in the list on p. 81, under 2) and 5).

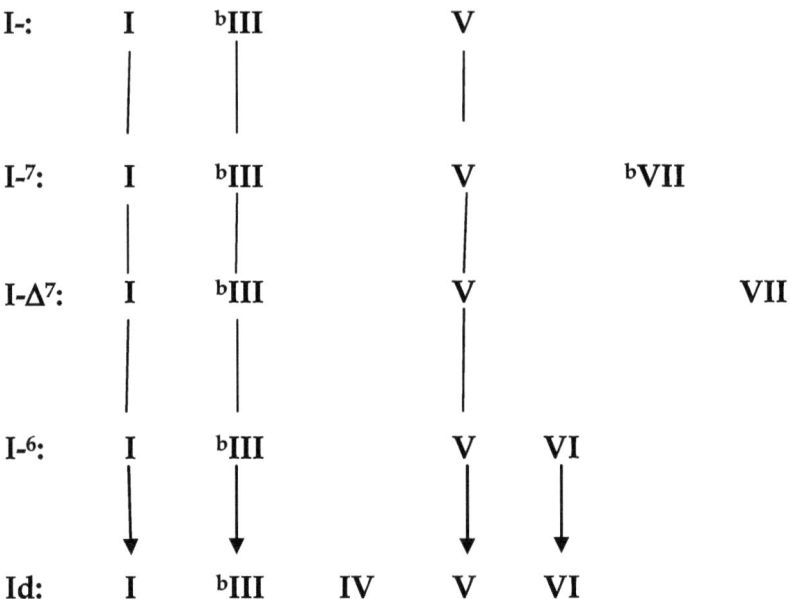

We see the only chord notes not represented by the scale **Id** are ᵇVII and
VII. In a way, the scale does not 'decide' which 7th to choose, **minor** or
major.

To sum up, in order to improvise on this chord progression, we use the
corresponding scale progression **IIo(7) - IIo(7) - Id**.

Comparing the situation with that of the corresponding major
progression, we see the similarity:

	maj situation	min situation
chord progression	II-⁷ - V⁷ - IΔ⁷	IIo⁷ - V⁷ᵇ⁹ - I-Δ⁷
scale progression	IIp - IId - IΔ⁷⁹	IIo(7) - IIo(7) - Id

This similarity is another reason why I prefer **IΔ⁷⁹**, rather than **Vmd**, as a
scale representation in the major case (see the discussion on p. 42 ff).

Minor II-V-I Chord Progressions

As an example for the min situation, we consider the progression:

$$Fo^7 - B^{b7b9} - E^b\text{-}\Delta^7$$

Our corresponding scale progression is then

$$Fo(7) - Fo(7) - E^bd:$$

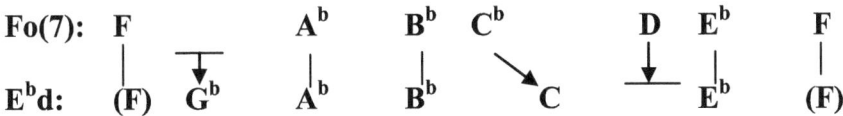

Thus, the dissolution here consists of inserting **G**^{b}, omitting **D**, and raising **C**^{b} to **C**. It is possible to keep **F** as an additional note. That is to say, we actually use the hexatonic **E**^{b}**d(9)**.
b) Another possible strategy is to step up a **min 3rd**, as we did in the previous chapter, and to use **IVo(7)** on the first 2 chords instead. We then have the scale progression:

$$IVo(7) - IVo(7) - Id$$

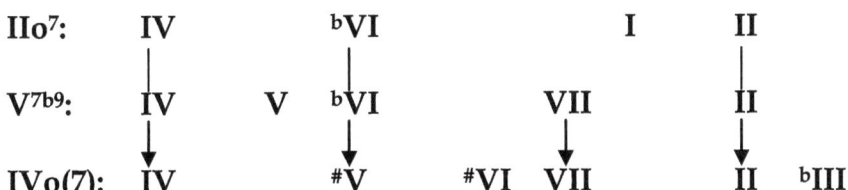

We see that **IVo(7)** represents the 2 chords well.* Two chord notes are

*consulting chap. 6 (see the list on p. 81) we find IVo among the eigenscales of V^7 (the transition V = I' gives us V^7 = I'^{7} and IVo = ^{b}VII'o, the latter of which is indeed an eigenscale of I'^{7}), but not among those of IIo^7 (the transition II = I' gives us IVo = ^{b}III'o, which is not an eigenscale of I'o^7). This shows us that a scale which is a good interpretation of a chord, must not necessarily be one of its eigenscales.

missing, **I**, the **7** of **IIo^7**, and **V**, the root of **V^{7b9}**. Which is no drama, because there is no law that every note of a chord must necessarily be present in a solo. On the contrary, it can be a stylistic means to use 'chord extensions' (the notes of a scale that are not the chord notes). This was largely done in the bebop era and can be considered a means of distinction between bebop and the previous swing era; during which the use of arpeggios of the underlying chords was rather common. – There are 2 scale notes in **IVo(7)**, **^{b}III** and **$^\#$VI**, which are not part of one of the chords; but they add an interesting colour, **^{b}III** being the altered note **^{b}9** of **IIo^7** and the **^{b}13** of **V^{7b9}**, **$^\#$VI** being the altered note **$^\#$5** of **IIo^7** and the **$^\#$9** of **V^{7b9}**.

In our concrete example above (**Fo^7** – **B^{b7b9}** – **E^b-Δ^7**) the scale progression is:

$$\mathbf{A^bo(7) - A^bo(7) - E^bd}$$

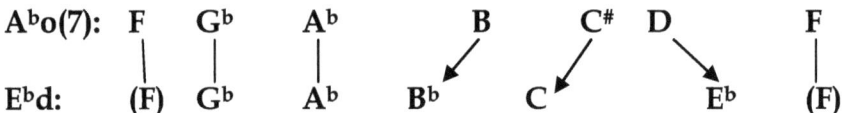

Thus, here the dissolution consists of flattening **B** and **D^b** to **B^b** and **C**, as well as raising **D** to **E^b**. It makes sense to use **E^{b}d(9)** here too.

It might be interesting that were one to put the 2 scales under 1) and 2), **IIo(7)** and **IVo(7)**, together, a new scale emerges. This scale is found in some books as the **'Spanish Scale'**:

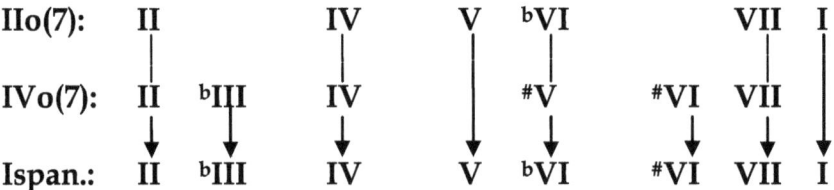

In order to give 'flesh' to these 'bones', let's study the situation for our concrete example **I = E^b**. Then **II = F**, **IV = A^b**, and we have:

Minor II-V-I Chord Progressions

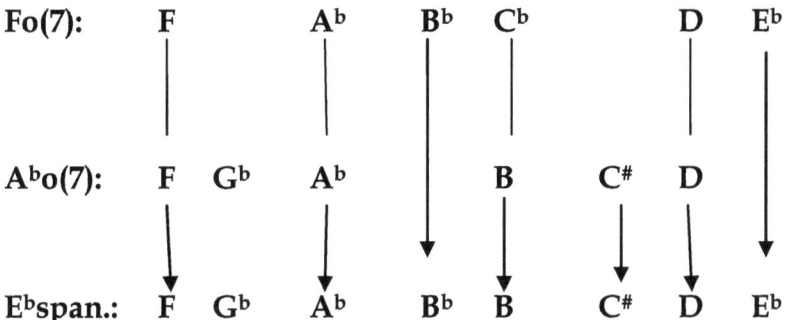

Fo(7):	F		A♭	B♭	C♭		D	E♭
A♭o(7):	F	G♭	A♭		B	C#	D	
E♭span.:	F	G♭	A♭	B♭	B	C#	D	E♭

To choose **E♭** as the root of this scale makes sense, as, examining it closer, we see that in this case it is **identical** with **E♭hmi, C# (= ♭VII) added**. This is of course not a genuine scale in our sense, as it is partly chromatic. In my opinion, it also should not be used in a chromatic way, just moving up and down through the notes. I suggest you split it into our 2 o-pentatonics and use them simultaneously, as soon as you master them both. For example, start a phrase in one scale and smoothly switch into the other.

c) There are more possibilities, of course. All the scales we considered in the major case containing altered notes we can use here on $V^{7(♭9)}$, too. This amounts to using scale progressions of 3 elements instead of 2. We start with either **IIo(7)** or **IVo(7)**, skip to one of the altered scales over $V^{7(♭9)}$, then dissolve to **Id**. Let's list the possible scale progressions (see the list of eigenscales of $I^{7♭9}$ in chap. 7, p. 89):

II/IVo(7) - ♭VImmi - Id

II/IVo(7) - ♭IIIhma - Id

II/IVo(7) - IVdim - Id

Summary

List of possible scale progressions to be played on **minor II-V-I progressions:**

II/IVo(7) - II/IVo(7) - Id

II/IVo(7) - ♭VImmi - Id

II/IVo(7) - ♭IIIhma - Id

II/IVo(7) - IVdim - Id

II/IVo(7) - ♭Vdim - Id

In the case of fast changing progressions, I recommend to use the first scale progression from the list, shortened to

II/IVo(7) – Id.

Unrelated Chords

And how to Treat Them in Improvisation

In some jazz standards, or parts of them, you find what I call 'unrelated chords', chords that are not recognizably part of a progression. A well-known example is Miles Davis' 'So What'. The A-part consists of the single chord D^{47}, in the B-part this rises a half step to the single chord Eb^{47}.

The general rule in such cases is to choose whatever scales you like from the list of eigenscales related to the chord. This even holds true for chords that are part of a progression, though there are simpler devices for the treatment of chord progressions. We discussed some of them in the two previous chapters.

In addition to this general rule, I would like to list the 'first choices', the pentatonics (in some cases: hexatonics, or scales) most frequently used in such cases. These are the pentatonics which are usually most closely related to the chords in question.

1) Io: Io(7)

2) Io⁷: ᵇIIId

3) I-⁷: Ip

4) I-Δ⁷: Id

5) I⁷: Vd

6) IΔ^7: Vmd

7) I+Δ^7: VIId(^{b}9)

9) Iø^7: VId(^{b}9)

10) I+^{7}: Vd(^{b}9)

11) IoΔ^7: ^{b}Vo

12) IøΔ^7: VId(9)

13) I^{47}: ^{b}VIImma

14) I$^4\Delta^7$: Id

I must admit, there are no strict rules why I chose exactly these scales. Nevertheless, they all sound good if played against the chords in question. Try it out! If you prefer different ones, make up your own list!

Unrelated Chords

It is interesting to note that I chose the pentatonic **Xd,** or a hexatonic extension of it, in **8 of 13 cases**! It shows what a useful tool this scale is, how many different colours it can express. In **2 cases** the choice was **Xo** or a hexatonic extension of it, while both **Xp** and **Xmd** are used only **once.** This shows how closely related they are to the chords they interpret, **I-⁷** in the case of **Ip** and **IΔ⁷** in the case of **Vmd.** In only one case I suggest the use of a whole cnc-scale, **ᵇVIImma** over **I⁴⁷**. This chord is open to the use of many scales, as we already saw (p. 83, 13)). My advice is to use those possibilities and to skip freely from one scale to another, improvising over this chord.

In some other cases (generally the minor chords) I could also have suggested the use of a cnc-scale, **ᵇIIImmi** over **Io⁷**, **ᵇVIImma ('I Dorian')** over **I-⁷**, and **Immi** over **I-Δ⁷**. Finally, in one case I could have suggested 2 complete scales over a major chord, **Vmmi** and **ᵇIImmi** (the 'altered scale') over **I⁷**, as we saw in chap. 7. George Russell would suggest **Vmma ('I Lydian')** over **IΔ⁷**. **Xobl** is the one pentatonic from our list that is not used at all here.

On Free Improvisation

Imagine humanity at a certain point in the development of their language.

Imagine a group of humans sitting together at a common meal, not yet able to speak freely, mainly communicating by using fixed phrases. For example, someone says, 'pass me the meat, please'. Everybody would use this fixed phrase, no-one would come up with another sentence of a personal colour meaning the same, such as, 'dear, would you be so kind as to pass me the plate of that delicious meat again?'

Next, they might start to talk about the weather, again using fixed phrases in order to exchange the necessary information, for example 'it is cold today, the sun is shining, it is springtime, tomorrow it will be warmer.' – 'No, I think tomorrow it will be still cold.' – 'I do not think so.' – 'I think I am right, the sun is not strong.' etc...

This system of fixed phrases will be greatly enlarged as time goes by, new phrases being invented all the time by people with special linguistic talents. One day, the time will come when everybody's linguistic abilities are so far developed that free speech is possible, everybody forming new sentences spontaneously.

In music today, we seem to be at a similar point in the development of the musical language. Compare the using of fixed phrases to the performing of compositions by the sight-reading of scores. The composers play the role of the especially linguistically talented people, inventing new phrases all the time. To me, the freely improvising musicians of today seem to be the first people who conscientiously work on their ability to use the musical language without limitations.

In light of this, you may perhaps be able to throw your prejudices regarding free improvisation overboard, like, 'those guys just play for themselves. They have fun, but no-one can listen to their music, not to speak of enjoying it,' or, 'it's just a prolonged production of all sorts of noises and has nothing to do with the development of any harmonic or melodic ideas,' in case you have any. Certainly, since the 60s of the last century, when musicians first started to explore and develop free improvisational concepts, the 'atonal' approach in its various forms has been an important integral part of the free jazz movement. However, the continuation of the improvisational traditions has also always been present, especially in the music of those who started their careers in the pre-free jazz era, such as Ornette Coleman and John Coltrane.

Comparing music and language once more, 'atonality' in language would amount to producing sounds and noises instead of meaningful sentences, or to develop and use a phantasy language. Both concepts have been explored by experimental poets. The first ones were the members of the Dada movement after the first world war. Examples are their 'sound poems' ('Lautgedichte' in German), or the 'Ursonate' by Kurt Schwitters.

The comparison should make it clear that atonality is not the only existing road to free improvisation. Try to imagine a concert of the future as an equivalent of a relaxed and enjoyable conversation among friends. They would start, perhaps, to talk about the weather and cooking recipes, then go on to the cinema program of the week, to films and film directors in general. Perhaps this would remind one of the participants of a funny experience in his last holiday, which he would relate at length, and later on they might all find themselves delving in the deep grounds of philosophy. None of this would have been prepared in any way, by scripts or a list with the conversation themes of the evening or whatever. Yet, someone reading this conversation afterward would not be able to decide if it was a continuous flow of free speech, or a conversation thought up and constructed by an author. Well, you might argue, 'a carefully constructed conversation in a work of fiction will generally be more to the point, more balanced in its content and vocabulary.' I would respond, 'maybe, but not necessarily always. Even a very good author will have difficulties to match the liveliness and direct energy of a real conversation in his writing.'

It is not my intention, though, to maintain that all concerts of the future will be the equivalent of a free conversation. The ability to communicate with spontaneously constructed sentences does not prevent people from gathering in meetings from time to time and sitting there, without uttering a single word, listening to one person reading from a book.

My own musical education, though for long years I was a rock musician, always included the experience of listening intently to musicians improvising freely. It was mainly Coltrane's music which opened my ears to free improvisation. Unfortunately, I never heard him play live. When he died, I was only 13 and had not even discovered rock music yet. However, in the 70s I studied some of his records and they inspired me to visit free jazz concerts. I had ample opportunity to do so, living in Berlin. Clubs like the Quartier Latin, the Flöz, and the foyer of the Akademie der Künste regularly featured free improvisers. The 'Total Music Meeting' was held annually, organized by the label 'Free Music Production'. Of all the many musicians whose concerts I attended back in those days, the strongest and most lasting impressions I received from the Enrico Rava quartet featuring Roswell Rudd, which I saw once at one of the Total Music Meetings, and from Gunter Hampel, who used to perform for 5 consecutive nights at the Flöz. When that took place, I went there every night. It was so intense, especially once, when the American clarinetist Perry Robinson formed part of Hampel's 'Galaxy Dream Band'. He, Hampel on bass clarinet, and two other reed players whose names I have forgotten used to play unaccompanied collective improvisations which lasted for what seemed like hours. I remember attending one of these performances in the company of a fellow musician; afterward, he just laughed and said, 'they are crazy'. I couldn't discern if this comment was meant to be a derision or a complement.

Much later, in a biography of Coltrane, I found myself very satisfyingly studying the tradition of other jazz musicians who had made sure to attend each concert when Coltrane had performed with Thelonious Monk in New York, in the early 60s.

To me, Gunter Hampel is a good example for a musician exploring the possibilities of free improvisation without denying jazz and also diverse other traditions, being the prolific composer that he is.

Once in these years, I also heard clarinetist Theo Jörgensmann play. Interestingly, I cannot recall any details of this concert. This is strange, in the light of the fact that today Jörgensmann, with whom I collaborate for years now, certainly is my main musical influence. It could not have been much different. Meeting him was to meet a man concentrating on one instrument, the clarinet, and one musical challenge, free improvisation, for more than 40 years now. The ideas developed here are strongly influenced by the many talks we had together (large parts of which were monologues by him) over the last years.

Analysis of a Bebop Theme (Donna Lee)

in terms of the pentatonic approach

Before studying concrete chord progressions, I would like to interpret this well-known tune by Miles Davis (ironically attributed to Charlie Parker) in the light of the Pentatonic Approach.

I chose this tune as it is a very sophisticated melody. You might ask yourself if you, as an improviser, could come up with melodic ideas in a solo similar to those used in the construction of this theme.

My answer is positive; yes, you can. All the phrases of the theme can be interpreted as being constructed from the different kinds of pentatonics (and their hexatonic extensions) I defined in chapter 5.

Let's see how this is done.*

The first phrase consists of 3 parts:

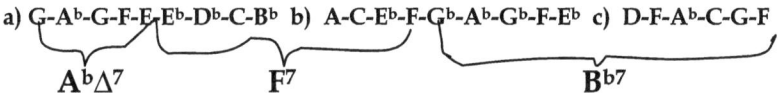

a) G-A$^\flat$-G-F-E-E$^\flat$-D$^\flat$-C-B$^\flat$ b) A-C-E$^\flat$-F-G$^\flat$-A$^\flat$-G$^\flat$-F-E$^\flat$ c) D-F-A$^\flat$-C-G-F

A$^\flat\Delta^7$ F^7 B$^{\flat7}$

part a) The notes **G, A$^\flat$, E$^\flat$, C,** and **B$^\flat$** form the pentatonic **E$^\flat$md.**

E$^\flat$md: E$^\flat$ G   A$^\flat$ B$^\flat$ C

This is the usual interpretation of the chord **A$^\flat\Delta^7$**, the opening chord of the tune. **E** and **F** are transitional notes between **G** and **E$^\flat$**, **D$^\flat$** is a transitional note between **E$^\flat$** and **C** (the phrase is descending). In fact, the whole **A$^\flat$mma**-scale is employed in a), as **F** and **D$^\flat$** complete **E$^\flat$md** to **A$^\flat$mma**; but I prefer to see the two notes rather as transitional notes. Both notes fall on a 'weak' offbeat, and **D$^\flat$** is the, meanwhile familiar, 'problematic' note over **A$^\flat\Delta^7$** (The whole scale, **A$^\flat$mma(E)** or **Imma(#5)**, has been called the 'bebop scale' by some scale theorists).

The last 4 notes are already played on the next chord of the tune, **F^7**. It is

*For copyright reasons, I did not reprint the theme here. You can use any Real Book copy of the tune for comparison. For our purposes, it will suffice to consider the chord progression and the tonal content of the theme phrases.

common improvisational practice that the melodic changes precede or delay the harmonic changes a little.

part b) The notes **A, C, E♭, F, G♭,** and **A♭** form the hextatonic **E♭o(9)**, a very common interpretation of **F⁷**, over which it is played here (see p. 100, c). We suggested **E♭o(7)** there: **V = F, IV = E♭**).

E♭o(9):   E♭   F   G♭   A♭   A   C,

The last 5 notes are again already played on the following chord, **B♭⁷**.

part c) **D, F, Ab, C,** and **G,** all belong to the hexatonic **Fd(9)**, another very common interpretation of **Bb⁷**, over which it is played (p. 100, a); **II = F**)

Fd(9):   F   G   A♭   B♭   C   D,

The second phrase consists of 5 parts:

a) E-D   **b)** E♭-A-B♭-D♭-F-A♭-C-E♭   **c)** D♭-E-F-C   **d)** B-F♯-E-D♯-C♯

  B♭⁷   B♭-7   E♭⁷

e) C-E♭-G-B♭-A♭

   A♭Δ⁷

part a) E and D still belong to **B♭7** (♯11 and 3) and should just be interpreted as a 'chromatic enclosure' of the **E♭** opening to the b) part of the phrase.

part b) E♭, B♭, D♭, F, A♭, and C form **B♭p(9)**, the usual interpretation of the underlying chord **B♭-7**, the first chord of a **maj II-V-I** progression here (chapter 9). **A** is a transitional note and opens an upward chord arpeggio of **B♭-7⁹**, a typical bebop phrase.

B♭p(9):   B♭   C   D♭   E♭   F   A♭

part c) D♭, E, F, and C all belong to **Go(7)**, one of the scales we listed in chapter 9 e) as a suitable choice for E^{b7}, the underlying chord here (E^b being the V of the progression, G becomes VII).

Go(7):   G B^b C D^b E   F

part d) **B, F#, E, D#,** and **C#,** all are part of **Bhma***, a scale that is generated by, and therefore also contains, **C#o(7)**:

C#o(7):   C#   E   F#   G   A#   B

Bhma: C#   D#   E   F#   G   A#   B

$C^{\#}o(7)$ is another of the suggested scales for E^{b7} (p. 100 c), with $V = E^b$ and $IV = D^b = C^{\#}$). So, with c) and d) we have here two different interpretations of one chord, E^{b7}, in a very short segment of space and time.

Go(7):   G B^b C D^b E   F

C#o(7):   G   A#   B   C#   E   F#

Comparing these two scales, we see that both contain the tetrachord **Go;** however, the two additional notes (**C** vs. **B,** and **F** vs. **F#**) are, in a way, exactly 'anti-symmetric'.

This is perhaps the most sophisticated part of the theme. To make a similarly quick change of interpretation while improvising does indeed afford considerable skill, but don't let that discourage you. Fully understanding a concept is the first step in the direction of being able to use it!

part e) The last part of the phrase, **C, E^b, G, B^b,** and **A^b,** marks the resolution, interpreting **$A^b\Delta^7$,** the **I** of the progression, and, like in a), we use

*Another scale containing these notes is **Emmi,** the altered scale of E^{b7}. The downward-moving phrase F#-E-D#-C# over E^{b7}, ending on C, the 3rd of the resolution $A^b\Delta$ (in general, expressed in chord notes, **#9-b9-1-7** over V^7, ending on the 3 of $I\Delta^7$), is a frequently used one in improvisations over **maj II-V-I** and is part of the scales in our list belonging to $I'^7\backslash 5$ ($I' = V$) in chap. 7: **^{b}VI'hma, bVII'dim, ^{b}II'mmi** (see p. 88).

E♭md: E♭   G A♭   B♭   C

The third phrase consists of 2 parts:

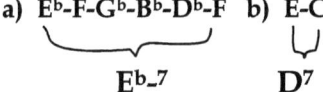

a) E♭-F-G♭-B♭-D♭-F b) E-C

E♭₋7   D⁷

part a) The notes of the first part all belong to **E♭p(9)**, the usual interpretation of **E♭-7**, the underlying chord and the first of a **II-♭II-I** progression here (♭II substituting **V** in already familiar fashion).

E♭p(9):   E♭   F G♭   A♭   B♭   D♭,

part b) E and C are the **9** and **7** of **D⁷**, the second chord of the progression. They can be interpreted as part of a common interpretation of **D⁷, Ad.**

The fourth phrase is short:

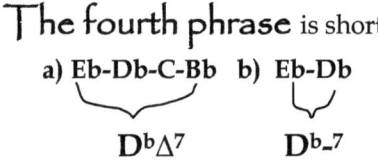

a) Eb-Db-C-Bb b) Eb-Db

D♭Δ⁷   D♭₋7

The chord belonging to a), **D♭Δ⁷** is the **I** of our last **II-V-I-progression**. However, if we consider it part of the progression **D♭Δ⁷ - D♭-7 - A♭Δ⁷**, we are dealing here with a kind of 'hidden **II-V-I-progression**'. **D♭Δ⁷** may be interpreted as a substitution for **B♭-7**, consisting of the same notes as **B♭-79** without the root **B♭**:

B♭₋79:   B♭   C D♭   F   A♭

D♭Δ⁷: C D♭   F   A♭

Analysis of a Bebop Theme

$D^{b\text{-}7}$ can sometimes have the function of a substitution for an altered E^{b7}-chord, consisting of the E^{b7} chord notes **7, ♭9, 11,** and **#5:**

$D^{b\text{-}7}$:	D^b		E	A^b		B
E^{b7} chord notes	7		♭9	11		#5
E^{b7}:	D^b	E^b	G		B^b	

In light of this, we have here $D^b\Delta^7$ - $D^{b\text{-}7}$ - $A^b\Delta^7$ as a substitution for $B^{b\text{-}7}$ – E^{b7} - $A^b\Delta^7$.

part a) The notes all form part of **B^bp(9),** interpreting the substitution of **$B^{b\text{-}7}$.**

part b) D^b and E^b are also part of part a) of the next phrase, interpreting the same chord $D^{b\text{-}7}$.

The 5th phrase is a long, 5-part phrase:

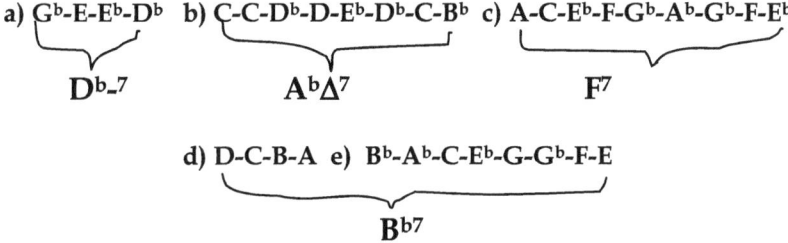

a) G^b-E-E^b-D^b b) C-C-D^b-D-E^b-D^b-C-B^b c) A-C-E^b-F-G^b-A^b-G^b-F-E^b

$D^{b\text{-}7}$ $A^b\Delta^7$ F^7

d) D-C-B-A e) B^b-A^b-C-E^b-G-G^b-F-E

B^{b7}

part a) The chord here is still $D^{b\text{-}7}$ as a substitution of E^{b7}, and the phrase is nearly identical with phrase 2 d), the notes (in the form F#-E-D#-C# there) being part of **Bhma** (see phrase 2 d), including the foot note).

part b) C, E^b, and B^b form part of E^b**md,** interpreting the chord here, $A^b\Delta^7$, in the usual way; D^b and D are transitional notes.

part c) Tonally identical with phrase 1b), and over the same chord (see phrase 1 b).

part d) D, C, B, and A all belong to **G♭dim,** the 'Coltrane scale' of **B♭7** (compare p. 99), g); here **I = E♭, V = B♭, ♭III = G♭**)

part e) All the notes here, except **E♭** and **G♭,** form part of **Fmmi,** one of the possible interpretations of **B♭7** (see p. 81, 5)). **G♭** is a transitional note between **G** and **F,** and **E♭** (a problematic note over **B♭7**) could well be replaced by **D** here. Note that the first 5 notes of part e) form the chord **A♭Δ79** and are a common bebop 'lick'. If you replace **E♭** with **D** the lick changes to **B♭-A♭-C-D-G** and forms the chord **A♭øΔ79,** part of **Fmmi.**

Fmmi: F   G A♭   B♭   C   D   E

Note the interesting note sequel **B-A-B♭-A♭** at the end of d) and beginning of e). Two descending w.s. **B-A** and **B♭-A♭,** a h.s. apart from each other, are used here. The first is part of **Adim,** the second of **Fmmi,** two different interpretations of **B♭7!** This is again a quite sophisticated section of the tune.

The 6ᵗʰ phrase consists of 3 parts:

a) E♭-D♭-F-A♭-C-B♭-F-G-A♭ b) G-B♭-D♭-B♭ c) E-G♭-E-E♭-D♭-C

B-♭7   E♭7   A♭Δ7

part a) The underlying chord is **B♭-7,** the notes form the complete scale **A♭mma,** a legitimate extension of the usual **B♭p** here. (On a **II-7** chord, you can generally extend **IIp** to **Imma** if you like, without coming across problematic notes. In the language of scale theory **Imma** is called 'II Dorian'.)

part b) **G, B♭,** and **D♭** form part of **B♭d,** a common interpretation of **E♭7.**

part c) Nearly identical with phrases 2 d) and 5 e), see above. The last note **C** belongs to **A♭Δ7.**

Analysis of a Bebop Theme

The 7th phrase is identical with the first.

The 8th phrase consists of 2 parts:

a) G-F-E-F-G-A♭-A-B♭-A-A♭-G **b)** D♭-E♭-D♭-C-B♭-A♭-B♭-A♭-G-E-F

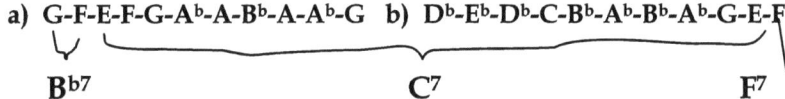

B♭7   **C7**   **F7**

part a) G, E, and B♭ belong to **Gd,** interpreting **C7** in the most common way. F, A♭ and A are transitional notes.

part b) D♭, E♭, C, B♭, A♭, G, and E belong to **A♭hma,** an extension of **B♭o(7),** another interpretation of **C7.** The last F belongs to the next chord, **F-7.**

The 9th phrase is, with 8 parts, the longest of the tune:

a) G-C-B-C-Db-D-Db-D-Eb **b)** E-Eb-E-Eb-D-Db-C-Bb

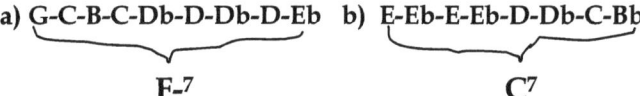

F-7   **C7**

c) Ab-Bb-Ab-G-Ab-G-F **d)** B-D-F-Ab-B-G-F-E **e)** Eb-Db-C-Bb

F-7   **Fo**   **A♭△7**

f) A-Gb-F-Eb **g)** Db-F-Ab-C **h)** Bb-Ab-G-Eb-Ab

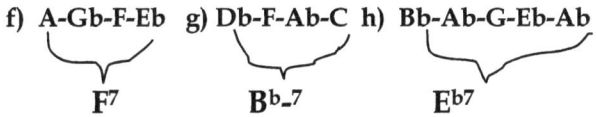

F7   **B♭-7**   **E♭7**

part a) The alternating chords **F-7** and **C7** belong to the minor **II-V-I** progression of **F-7.** As I suggested in the chapter about this progression, **Fd** would be the first choice for **F-7.** Of part a), only **G, C,** and **E♭** belong to **Fd(9),** all the other notes are transitional. This is an example of a very chromatic approach.

part b) E, D♭, C, and B♭ form part of **Go**, the first choice here for interpreting **C⁷**, but still very 'chromatically clouded'.

part c) A♭, B♭, G, and F form part of **Fd(9)**, interpreting **F-⁷**.

part d) The chord here, **Fo**, could be called a 'chameleon chord', as it may stand for any of the chords **E⁷♭⁹**, **G⁷♭⁹**, **B♭⁷♭⁹**, or **D♭⁷♭⁹**:

Fo:	F	A♭		C♭		D
E⁷♭⁹:	E F	G♯		B		D
G⁷♭⁹:	F	G A♭		B		D
B♭⁷♭⁹:	F	A♭	B♭	C♭		D
D♭⁷♭⁹:	F	A♭		B	C♯	D

The phrase here consists of **B, D, F, A♭, G,** and **E,** which form the hexatonic **Do(9)**.

Interpreting **Fo** as **G⁷♭⁹**, the most common resolution would be **C-**. The next chord in our tune, **A♭Δ⁷**, is a suitable substitution for **C-**. So, this interpretation does make good sense.

part e) E♭, C, and B♭ form part of **E♭md**, interpreting **A♭Δ⁷**.

part f) A, G♭, F, and E♭ form part of **Co**, interpreting **F⁷**.

part g) D♭, F, A♭, and C form part of **B♭p(9)**, interpreting **B♭-⁷**.

part h) Lastly, B♭, G, and E♭ form part of **B♭d**, interpreting **E♭7**. The last note, **A♭**, is the root of the resolving chord **A♭Δ⁷**.

Analysis of a Bebop Theme

I would like to add a comment to my analysis. I do not at all think that the pentatonic approach is the only possible way to interpret this tune, but I do think I was able to show that it helps to understand what is going on here harmonically and melodically. I must say, so far I have not found any book that would provide me with principles on how to achieve an improvisational style that would make me as cool-sounding as the 'Donna Lee' theme is. This is one of the reasons why I wrote this book.

An additional warning:

There is definitely the danger that you will eventually become a little bit too mechanical-sounding (on a high level, though) if you stick too closely to the principles described here. Keep in mind that you should always be open to the unexpected that your fingers, your temper, your mood, or whatever might influence your playing, has to offer. In the words of my colleague, the jazz clarinetist Theo Joergensmann, "a 'scientific' (or mathematical) approach (as the pentatonic approach certainly is) can never provide the full truth, it will always stay behind the full range of possibilities that exist."

To underline this, I want to state that I am certain it would be possible to write a computer program which combines the principles of the pentatonic approach, a vast library of rhythmical patterns of all kinds, and a device that produces notes by chance (while observing the principles). You would come up with a computer improvising admirably well, at least tonally. I don't believe this would be a challenge for human improvisers. A human improviser would always beat the computer in the field of producing drama in his solo, of creating suspense, humor, etc. However, it might be useful to listen to the improvising computer in order to learn something. I would be very curious to hear it play.

Examples

In this chapter, I try to apply the pentatonic approach to some classical and modern jazz-standards, as well as to music pieces of other stylistic realms.

Please keep in mind these are only suggestions. There is always more than one possible way to get interesting results.

Minor Blues

|| D-⁷ | % | % | % | G-⁷ | % | D-⁷ | % | A⁷ | % |
| D-⁷ | | A⁷ | |

The Minor Blues, in the key of D-, is a good tune for beginners. This is not only because you can **simply play one blues pentatonic over it** (the **D pentatonic** in case of the **D minor blues**), but also because you can go one little step further and **play 2 scales instead of 1**, **Dd** over **D-⁷** and **Eo(7)** over **A⁷** as well as **G-⁷**. Indeed, **Eo(7)** is a valid interpretation of **A⁷** as well as of **G-⁷**, E being the **V** of **A** (compare p. 81, 5)) and the **VI** of **G** (p. 81, 3); **VIo** is not an eigenscale of **I-⁷**, but can be completed to one, **Vhmi**; compare p. 165: **Ihmi** contains **IIo**).

The corresponding scale progression then looks like this:

|| Dd | % | % | % | Eo(7) | % | Dd | % | Eo(7) |
| % | Dd | % | |

As we have a slowly changing chord progression here, to take deviations into neighboring scales makes sense. For example to use **Do, Bo,** or **Fo** on **D-⁷**, and **Go(7)** or **B♭mmi** on **A⁷** and **G-⁷**; never stop experimenting!

Dark Eyes

| | A⁷ | % | D- | % | A⁷ | % | D- | D⁷ | | G- | % |
| D- | % | | A⁷ | % | D- | % | |

Observe that, apart from **D⁷**, we have here the three chords of the Minor Blues in **D**   (D-, G-, A⁷). This would suggest to use the scales **Dd** over **D-**, and **Eo(7)** (as well as the altered scale **B♭mmi**) over **A⁷** and **G-** . Over **D⁷**, the **V** of **G-**, we could use the scale **Ao(7)**. The scale progression then becomes:

	Eo(7)/B♭mmi	%	Dd	%	Eo(7)/B♭mmi
%	Dd	Ao(7)		Eo(7)/B♭mmi	%	Dd	%	
	Eo(7)/B♭mmi	%	Dd	%	

Footprints

| | C⁴⁷ | % | % | % | F⁴⁷ | % | C⁴⁷ | % | F#⁴⁷ F⁷#¹¹ |
| E⁷alt A⁷alt | C⁴⁷ | % | |

Footprints is a minor 6/4 Blues in **C** by Wayne Shorter, using **X⁴⁷** chords instead of the usual minor chords and a row of rather complicated chords, which substituting the normally expected **G⁷** in bars 9 and 10.

The chord notation **'E⁷alt'** and **'A⁷alt'** is somewhat mysterious. It is generally used to indicate that any variation of **E⁷** and **A⁷** containing additional altered notes can be used here (**E⁷#⁹**, **E⁷♭⁹**, etc.) I would suggest to play the altered scales here, **Fmmi** over **E⁷** and **B♭mmi** over **A⁷**.

Examples

Let's have a closer look at the unusual part of the progression. If we interpret $F^{\#47}$ to be a **substitution** for $F^{\#-7}$, and $F^{7\#11}$ to be the **tritone substitution** for B^7, then we have a **familiar II-V progression with I = E** as the expected resolution. Only, we have E^7alt instead of $E\Delta^7$ as I in our progression (its root is a minor 3rd lower than the G^7 that we would expect here).

In the case of quickly changing 7th chords $II^7 - V^7$ (**II = E, V = A**), it is always convenient to interpret II^7 as a substitution for II^{-7}, which gives us 2 **II-V-progressions**:

$$| \ F^{\#-7} \ B^7 \ | \ E^{-7} \ A^7 \ |$$

with the possible scale progression:

$$| \ F^{\#}o(7) \ | \ Eo(7) \ |$$

A complete scale progression could then be:

$$|| \ Cd \ | \ \% \ | \ \% \ | \ \% \ | \ Do(7) \ | \ \% \ | \ Cd \ | \ \% \ |$$
$$| \ F^{\#}o(7) \ | \ Eo(7) \ | \ Cd \ | \ \% \ ||$$

Observe that **Eo(7)** would classically resolve to **Dd** instead of **Cd**.

Simone

$$|| \ D^{47} \ | \ E^{47} \ | \ D^{47} \ | \ Eb\emptyset^7 \ | \ D^{47} \ | \ E^{47} \ | \ A^{-7} \ | \ D^7 \ | \ G^{47} |$$
$$| \ A^{47} \ | \ Bb^{47} \ | \ Eb\emptyset^7 \ | \ D^{47} \ | \ E^{47} \ | \ F\Delta^7 \ | \ F^{\#47} \ | \ F^{-7} \ |$$
$$| \ Bb^7 \ | \ E^{-7} \ | \ A^7 \ | \ D^{47} \ | \ E^{47} \ | \ D^{47} \ | \ Eb\emptyset^7 \ ||$$

Simone, a jazz waltz by Frank Foster, has been described as difficult to improvise upon, because there is a different chord in each bar of the tune. However, these many changes are easier to 'digest' as you might guess. Indeed, it is a hidden 6/4 Minor Blues that we deal with here. The theme consists of 24 bars. The first 8 bars are dominated by **D minor** (1), the second 4 bars are dominated by **G minor** (2), then again 4 bars of **D minor** (3), followed by 4 bars dominated by **A⁷** (4), leading back to the **D minor** for the last 4 bars (5).

The details:

1) $\mathbf{|\ D^{47}\ |\ E^{47}\ |\ D^{47}\ |\ E^b\emptyset^7\ |\ D^{47}\ |\ E^{47}\ |\ A\text{-}^7\ |\ D^7\ |}$

D⁴⁷ and **E⁴⁷** can be considered equivalent to the chords **D-⁷** and **E-⁷**, the **II** and **III** of **Cmma (D Dorian)**. **E♭ø⁷** should then be interpreted as an altered substitution of **A⁷**, the **V** of **D-**. Bars 7 and 8 prepare, in II-V-I fashion, the rise to **G⁴⁷**, the substitution for the subdominant **G-⁷**.

2) $\mathbf{|\ G^{47}\ |\ A^{47}\ |\ B^{b47}\ |\ E^b\emptyset^7\ |}$

In a similar fashion as before, **G⁴⁷** and **A⁴⁷** are substituted for **G-⁷** and **A-⁷**, the **II** and **III** of **Fmma (G Dorian)**. **B♭⁴⁷** is substituted for **B♭-⁷**, the **II** of **(V) E♭ø⁷**, again replacing **A⁷**. The last 2 bars lead back to the Tonic **D⁴⁷**.

3) $\mathbf{|\ D^{47}\ |\ E^{47}\ |\ F\Delta^7\ |\ F^{\#47}\ |}$

The first 3 chords constitute the **II**, **III**, and **IV** of **Cmma**; the **4ᵗʰ** is the starting point of a chromatic descent to **A⁷**.

4) $\mathbf{(|\ F^{\#47}\ |)\ F\text{-}^7\ |\ B^{b7}\ |\ E\text{-}^7\ |\ A^7\ |}$

Indeed, if we consider **F#⁴⁷** to stand for **F#-⁷/B⁷**, we have 3 chromatically descending II-V progressions here, the last of them leading back to the Tonic.

The last 4 bars of the progression,

$$5) \mid D^{47} \mid E^{47} \mid D^{47} \mid E^{b}\varnothing^{7} \mid,$$

are identical with the first.

These considerations suggest that the following scale progression would be a suitable choice:

	Dd	%	%	B♭mmi (or Eo(7)	Dd	%	Ao
%	Gd	%	B♭d	B♭mmi/Eo(7)	Dd	%	%
F#d	Fd	%	Eo	%	Dd	%	%
B♭mmi/Eo(7)		.

Turnarounds (vertical approach)

In the chapter about horizontal playing, we used the turnaround progression

$$I\Delta^{7} - VI\text{-}^{7} - II\text{-}^{7} - V^{7}$$

as an example for the horizontal approach. Here, we explore how this progression can be interpreted vertically.

If we consider **VI-7** to be a substitution for **IΔ7**, the progression simplifies to

$$I\Delta^{7} - \% - II\text{-}^{7} - V^{7}.$$

This is the **maj II-V-I-progression** in reversed order, and we may apply here the ideas we discussed in chapter 9.

There are variations of the turnaround progression. The most frequent are,

$$1) \ I\Delta^{7} - VI^{7} - II\text{-}^{7} - V^{7},$$

the second chord being a maj instead of a min 7th chord, and

2) I^7 – VI^7 – II^{-7} – V^7.

I would like to call the second variation the '**Blues Turnaround**', because it is a fixed part of the usual major Blues progression which we will study later on.

In **case 1)**, we can consider IΔ^7 to be a substitution for **III-7**, and with **III-7** – **VI7** – **II-7** – **V7** we have 2 subsequent **II-V**-progressions. For example, take **I** to be **F**, then the progression, with the substitution of **A-7** for FΔ^7, is **A-7** – **D7** – **G-7** – **C7**. Here, we can also apply the ideas of chapter 9.

In **case 2)**, the second part of the progression remains the same as before (**II-7** – **V7**). As for the progression **I7** – **VI7**, observe that both chords belong to **IVhma** (**I7** and **VI7** being eigenchords of its 5th and 3rd degrees), which makes **Vo(7)** a reasonable substitution for both chords. This renders the scale progression **Vo(7)** - % - **IIp** – **IIo(7)**.

Even easier to remember, because the roots of the scales are closer together, is the progression **IIIo(7)** - % - **IIp** – **IIo(7)** which I recommend as the best option here. **IIIo** figures in the list of eigenscales of both **I7** and **VI7** (with **VI** = **I'**, we get **III** = **V'**).
A bit more complicated, but very vertical and therefore logical-sounding, is the scale progression **Vd(9)** - **IIIo(7)** - **IIp** – **IIo(7)**. Let's examine the transition from **Vd(9)** to **IIIo(7)** more closely:

Vd(9):	V	VI	♭VII	*I*	II	III

IIIo(7):	V	VI	♭VII	*#I*	II	III

You see, the transition just consists of raising **I** by a h.s. - If the turnaround is a half-bar progression (as is the case in the last 2 bars of a blues), then it is reasonable to shorten the scale progression to **IIIo(7)** - **IIo(7)**.

The Chord Progression $I^{-7} - {}^{b}VI^{7}$

Note that the 2 chords are never found in the same scale. ${}^{b}VI^{7}$ is the dominant major chord of either **${}^{b}IImma$, ${}^{b}IImmi$, ${}^{b}IIhma$,** or **${}^{b}IIhmi$;** or the 3rd degree of **IIIhma.** In the first 2 cases, the scales contain Io^{7} instead of **I-7,** in the second 2 case, **Io,** and in the last case, $I+\Delta^{7}$.

Nevertheless, there are 2 closely related scales, each of which contains one of the chords. **I-7** is an eigenchord of **${}^{b}IIImma$,** the parallel maj scale, while **${}^{b}VI^{7}$** is the 4th degree of **${}^{b}IIImmi$.** The 2 scales **${}^{b}IIImma$** and **${}^{b}IIImmi$** differ only in one note and are thus suitable candidates for the use in improvisation.

Let's consider the situation more closely:

I-7:	I		^{b}III		V		^{b}VII
^{b}IIImma:	I	II	^{b}III	IV	V	^{b}VI	^{b}VII
^{b}IIImmi:	I	II	^{b}III	IV	^{b}V	^{b}VI	^{b}VII
^{b}VI7:	I		^{b}III		^{b}V	^{b}VI	

We see that the scale progression **${}^{b}IIImma$ – ${}^{b}IIImmi$** nicely reflects the chord progression by mirroring exactly the important note change $V \rightarrow {}^{b}V$, leaving everything else unchanged.

Well, a simpler device is acceptable in this situation. If we stick to **${}^{b}IIImmi$** throughout the chord progression, we simply play the altered note **${}^{b}V$** (the **${}^{b}5$** of **I-7**) against the first chord.

In this case, the use of the full scales does not arouse any problems. Though, in light of our pentatonic approach, there is a fresher sounding alternative. We could use the progression consisting of the 2 pentatonics **Id** and **${}^{b}IIId$,** the two standard interpretations of the chords **I-7** and **${}^{b}VI^{7}$** (note that if **I' = ${}^{b}VI$,** then **${}^{b}III = V'$; V'd** being the standard interpretation of **I'7**).

Summary for the chord progression **I-⁷ – ᵇVI⁷:**

Simplest strategy: use **ᵇIIImmi** throughout the progression.

More vertical approach: use the corresponding scale progression **ᵇIIImma – ᵇIIImmi.**

Pentatonic approach: use the pentatonic progression **Id – bIIId.**

Examples:

1) Henry Mancini's famous **Pink Panther Theme** makes use of the chord progression.

| E-⁷ | % | C⁷ | % | E-⁷ | % | F⁷ | % | E-⁷ | % | | C⁷ | % | ...

The simplest strategy would be to play

| Gmmi | % | % | % | % | % | Cd | % | Gmmi | | % | % | % |,

Cd being the standard choice for **F⁷**, the tritone substitution of the dominant 7th of E-, **B⁷.**
However, the pentatonic progression would be more elegant:

| Ed | % | Gd | % | Ed | % | Cd | % | Ed | % | |Gd | % | ...

2) The tune **Frog Dance** by Barbara Dennerlein is a 12-bar blues-like 6/8 theme with a bass riff similar to that of Miles Davis' and Bill Evans' famous **All Blues**. The chord progression is:

Examples
_____

**| | F-⁷ | % | % | % | Db⁷ | % | F-⁷ | % | B⁷ | Bb⁷|
|F-⁷ | % | |**

The corresponding pentatonic progression would be:

**| | Fd | % | % | % | Abd | % | Fd | % | Gbd |
|Fd | % | % | |**

3) The B part of Jobim's **Girl From Ipanema** contains several I-⁷ – ᵇVI⁷ progressions:

**| | GᵇΔ⁷ | % | B⁷ | % | Gᵇ-⁷ | % | D⁷ | % | G-⁷ |
|% |Eᵇ⁷ | % | A-⁷ | |D⁷ | G-⁷ | C⁷ | |**

Bars 5-8 form a I-⁷ – ᵇVI⁷ progression with I = Gᵇ, and bars 9-12 do the same with I a h.s. higher. Bars 1 and 2 form something you could call a 'hidden I-⁷ – ᵇVI⁷ progression', if you interpret GᵇΔ⁷ to be a substitution for the parallel minor chord Eb-⁷, with I = Eᵇ, which indeed makes sense. Playing the pentatonic progression Eᵇd – Gᵇd sounds good here (try it out!).

In more detail, we have:

$G^b\Delta^7$:	G^b		B^b		D^b		F
		9		#11		13	
E^bd:	G^b	A^b	B^b	C		E^b	

Thus, E^bd contains, besides the chord notes G^b and B^b, the chord extensions **9, #11**, and **13**.

The complete pentatonic progression corresponding to the B part of 'Girl From Ipanema' could now look like this:

**|| E^bd | % | G^bd | % | % | % | Ad | % | Gd |
|% |B^bd | % | Ap | Ao | Gp | Go ||,**

The last 4 bars being the 2 consecutive **maj II-V-I** progressions starting with **A-7** and **G-7,** respectively.

By the way, talking about the B part of the song, we should not go on without discussing its A part as well. Its chord progression is:

**|| $F\Delta^7$ | % | G^7 | % | G-7 | G^{b7} | $F\Delta^7$ | G^{b7} | $F\Delta^7$ |
|% |G^7 | % | G-7|G^{b7} | $F\Delta^7$ | % ||**

G^{b7} in bar 6 is the tritone substitution for C^7. I recommend to play **Go** and **D^{b}mmi** alternatively over it. They are 2 of the scales suggested in chapter 9 for C^7, and **Go** contains, with respect to G^{b7}, the altered notes $^b9$ and $^b5$; while G^{b7} is even an eigenchord of **D^{b}mmi**. With the latter scale, the scale progression looks like this:

**|| Cmd | % | Dd | % | Gp | D^{b}mmi | Cmd |
| D^{b}mmi | Cmd | % |Dd | % | Gp |D^{b}mmi |
|Cmd |% ||**

Examples

The following **2 extensions** of the progression I-7 – ♭VI7 you will meet in some situations:

$$I_{-7} - ^{\flat}VI^7 - V^7$$

and

$$I_{-7} - ^{\flat}VII^7 - ^{\flat}VI^7 - V^7$$

1) I-7 – ♭VI7 – V7: As **V7** is the dominant of **I-7**, the most straightforward scale choice is **IIo(7)**, which renders the scale progression **Id – ♭IIId – IIo(7)**.

2) I-7 – ♭VII7 – ♭VI7 – V7: Choosing the most common interpretation of ♭VII, **IVd**, we obtain **Id – IVd - ♭IIId – IIo(7)** .

Examples of this progression are the A-part of '**Song For My Father**' by Horace Silver with **I = F** (F-7 – E♭7 – D♭7 – C7), '**Hit The Road Jack**' by Ray Charles with **I = A** (A-7 – G7 – F7 – E7), or '**Round Midnight**' by Thelonious Monk, in which a variant of it forms part of the B-part with **I = E♭** (E♭7 – D♭7 – B7 – B♭7, see discussion below).
In the case of the Ray Charles' tune, a horizontal approach is required due to the quick half-bar changes:

$$|\ A_{-7}\ G^7\ |\ F^7\ E^7\ |$$

A horizontal approach that works is to consider **A-7** and **G7** as part of **Cmma** and play **Ap** in the first bar.
The scale we use on **E7** here, **Bo(7)**, also fits **F7** quite well except that it has **Δ7** instead of **7**, an acceptable compromise for the quickly changing progression:

F⁷:	**F**		**A**	**C**	**E♭**	
	root	♭3 3		#11	13	Δ7
Bo(7):	**F**	**G#**	**A**	**B**	**D**	**E**

This gives us the scale progression | **Ap** | **Bo(7)** |, which is quite similar to the familiar progression **IIo(7) – Id** we use in the case of quickly changing **minor II-V-I progressions.** The theme of the tune employs only the **A Blues pentatonic.**

Another extension you often find in Rock tunes is:

I- - ♭VII – ♭VI – (♭VII)

In this progression, we usually just deal with the triads, the 7ᵗʰs are generally omitted. There is a vast range of songs which have employed this progression throughout the decades, from Bob Dylan's 'All Along The Wachtower' (I = D) and the last part of Led Zeppelin's 'Stairway To Heaven', to the outro of the Red Hot Chili Pepper's 'Under The Bridge' (I = A in the 2 latter cases) or 'Schrei nach Liebe' by Die Ärzte (I = D).
As the 7ᵗʰs of the chords are not specified, we can just identify **I-, ♭VII,** and **♭VI** as eigenchords of **♭IIImma** (6ᵗʰ, 5ᵗʰ, and 4ᵗʰ degree respectively) and play

Ip

on the whole progression (the horizontal approach). For example, in **'Under The Bridge'**, the exact progression of the outro is:

| A A- | G F |

So, we play **Ap** everywhere. The short half-bar appearance of the maj triad **A** is not a problem here. Playing **C**, the min 3ʳᵈ of **Ap,** against the maj 3ʳᵈ, **C#**, gives us the usual Blue Note effect.

Note that playing **Ap** on **F** causes us to interpret this triad as **FΔ⁷** rather than **F⁷**, as **Ap** contains **E**, the **Δ⁷** of **F**, while the **7, E♭**, is the additional Blue Note of **Ap.**

Major Blues (B^b)

We consider the chord progression:

| | Bb7 | Eb7 | Bb7 | % | Eb7 | Eo | Bb7 | G7 | C-7 |
| F7 | Bb7 G7 | C-7 F7 | |

This 12-bar-structure is an elaboration of a simpler 3-chord-structure of this form:

| | Bb7 | % | % | % | Eb7 | % | Bb7 | % | F7 | Eb7 |
| Bb7 | F7 | |

This is a popular progression for beginners because it is suitable for the use of just one scale, the B^b Blues pentatonic, thus being a good example of horizontal improvising.

However, against the more elaborate Blues scheme above, the use of just this one scale has an acoustic effect similar to the optical one of painting a complete 6-piece-flat, kitchen, bathroom, and the interior of all cupboards and wardrobes included, with just one colour. If this colour was red, the outcome might look like a work of wild and mind-disturbing art. In the case of the Blues pentatonic, it definitely doesn't sound like any such thing.

So, let's be a little bit more imaginative and use a different colour at least in the bathroom, kitchen, cupboards, and wardrobes. This will lead us to what we could call:

the semi-horizontal approach

The semi-horizontal approach will provide us with quite authentic, bluesy-sounding phrases. Our **main colour** will not be the B^b Blues pentatonic, but instead the **G Blues pentatonic**:

Gp: G B♭ (C) D♭ D F G

Note that normally we write the Blue Note, **D♭**, in brackets, and here **C** instead. With this, I want to suggest that you should emphasize **D♭** more strongly than **C** in your playing. By doing so, you simultaneously make use of the maj **3ʳᵈ D** and the min **3ʳᵈ D♭** when you come to the root chord, **B♭⁷**, which results in giving your phrases an authentic Blues colour.

The last 6 bars of the Blues progression are just 2 consecutive 'Blues-turnarounds' (see above), one whole-bar, | **B♭ ⁷** | **G⁷** | **C-⁷** | **F⁷** |, and one half-bar turnaround, | **B♭⁷ G⁷** | **C-⁷ F⁷** |. Here, the use of **Gp** also makes perfect sense (see p. 93 ff). The only difference between the 'Blues' turnaround and the 'normal' turnaround is that in the former case the first chord is **B♭⁷**, in the latter **B♭Δ⁷**. Note that in both cases you can use **Gp**, because it contains neither the **maj 7ᵗʰ**, **A**, nor the **min 7ᵗʰ**, **A♭**. In fact, seen as a chord, **Gp** is identical with the **B♭ maj triad**, with the chord extensions **9** and **13** added:

B♭:	**B♭**		**D**	**F**	
	root	9	3	5	13
Gp:	**B♭**	**C**	**D**	**F**	**G ,**

Hence, it can be played over both **B♭⁷** and **B♭Δ⁷**.

The chord **B♭⁷** and the **Blues-turnaround** together cover three quarters of the Blues progression (bars 1, 3, 4, and bars 7 to 12). This leaves us with just 3 bars calling for a colour different from Gp, bars 2, 5, and 6. Here, we find the chords **E♭⁷** and **Eo**. Note that **Eo** can be interpreted as **E♭⁷♭9** (which equals Eo, with added root E♭; compare chapter 13, p. 126, the discussion of phrase 9, part d;). This means that bars 2, 5, and 6 are basically occupied by the 4ᵗʰ degree of the B♭-Blues, namely **E♭⁷**. A well-fitting colour here is the usual **B♭d** (= E♭⁷9), except for bar 5, with **Eo**, where we should use the slightly different **B♭o** (= E♭⁷♭9).

Note that **B♭d** can be interpreted as the chord **B♭-11/13**, the **B♭ min triad** with the chord extensions **11** and **13**:

	root	♭3	11	5	13
B♭-11/13:	**B♭**	**D♭**	**E♭**	**F**	**G**

In the same manner, we regard **B♭o** (the pentatonic) to be the chord **B♭o$^{11/13}$**:

	root	♭3	11	♭5	13
B♭o$^{11/13}$:	**B♭**	**D♭**	**E♭**	**F♭**	**G**

The result of these considerations is that we can re-interpret the B♭-Blues chord progression thus (omitting the chord extensions for the sake of clarity):

|| B♭ | B♭- | B♭ | % | B♭- | B♭o | B♭ | % | % | % | |% | % ||

In this view, a Blues is basically an oscillation between the major and the minor triad of its root.

In terms of pentatonics, the corresponding scale progression looks like this:

|| Gp | B♭d | Gp | % | B♭d | B♭o | Gp | % | % | |% | |% | % ||

For a clearer view of the changes, let's relate the 3 scales to each other:

Gp:	**B♭**	**(C)**	**D♭**	**D**	**F**	**G**
B♭d:	**B♭**	**(C)**	**D♭**	**E♭**	**F**	**G**
B♭o:	**B♭**	**(C)**	**D♭**	**E♭** **F♭**		**G**
Gp:	**B♭**	**(C)**	**D♭**	**D**	**F**	**G**

We see, the transition from **Gp** to **B♭d** simply consists of raising **D** to **E♭**, while that from **B♭d** to **B♭o** consists of lowering **F** to **F♭** (**= E**). **C** can be inserted (as the 9) in both **B♭d** and **B♭o** without problems.

The Full Vertical Approach

As the Blues progression mainly consists of dominant 7th chords, there are many possibilities regarding the choice of scales. We are not going to list them all here. For a comprehensive overview just study the alteration possibilities for these type of chords in the chapter 7. Here, I show you only one way to paint your '6-piece-Blues-flat' in a set of lively, appealing colours (at least to me).

1) | B♭7 | E♭7 | B♭7 | % | E♭7 |

The first choice for the chords **B♭7** and **E♭7**, as we saw, are the scales **Fd,** and **B♭d**. We use them here in the first 3 bars, but in the 4th bar let us switch to one of the possible altered scales we can use on **B♭7**, **Fdim** (see chap. 9 f), p. 99; with **II = F**). The corresponding scale progression so far is then:

| Fd | B♭d | Fd | Fdim | B♭d |

2) | Eo |

Above, I suggested to use **B♭o** here; another possibility is **B♭dim**. The choice of this scale renders a certain symmetry in the form of the 2 similar progressions, **Fd-Fdim** and **B♭d-B♭dim**. The first half of the Blues scale progression then looks like this:

| Fd | B♭d | Fd | Fdim | B♭d | B♭dim |

3) | B♭7 | G7 | C-7 | F7 | B♭7 G7 | C-7 F7 |

Examples
___

We already saw that this second half of the Blues consists of **2 Blues turn-arounds, one whole-bar and one half-bar.** Our discussion of this progression above renders in this case:

| Fd | Do(7) | Cp | Co(7) | Do(7) | Co(7) |

So, the full scale progression looks like this:

| Fd | B♭d | Fd | Fdim | B♭d | B♭dim | Fd |
|Do(7) |Cp | Co(7) | Do(7) | |Co(7) |

7 different scales in 12 bars, isn't that horrifying??

Yes and no.

First of all, I would like to remind you, I'm discussing a full vertical approach here. Beforehand we were talking about much simpler improvisational devices that also work quite well in the same situation.

Then, the chord structure considered here is normally only employed in a slow or medium tempo. An up-tempo Blues usually consists of only 3 chords.

Third, all the scale transitions, **Fd-Fdim** or **Do(7)-Cp**, are very common in jazz standards, and are not special features of the Blues. Moreover, in these transitions only a few notes are being changed, the main body is left unchanged. So, it's worth rehearsing them, you'll be able to apply your abilities to many different situations.

Lastly, compare learning how to improvise to the learning of a new language. In such a practice you're bound to come, sooner or later, across quite complicated grammatical constructions. The only way to learn them is by talking, talking, and more talking. You start with simple sentences. Only after a considerable amount of time, will you be able to relate a whole story. The very same holds true for the use of musical language in improvisation.

Round Midnight

I'll give you the chord progression of this famous ballad and the corresponding scale progression in one scheme. The scales are noted between the bars, the chords underneath:

(A) | |: **Eᵇd** | **Fo** | **Eᵇp Eᵇo** | **Bd** **Bᵇo** |
  Eᵇ- Co⁷ Fo⁷ Bᵇ⁷ Eᵇ-7 Aᵇ⁷ B-7 E⁷ Bᵇ-7 Eᵇ⁷

|1.———————— |2.————————

| **Aᵇp Aᵇo** |**Eᵇp Eᵇo** | **Gᵇd**| **Fo** : | | **Gᵇd Fo** | **Eᵇd**|
  Aᵇ-7 Dᵇ⁷ Eᵇ-7 Aᵇ⁷ B⁷ Bᵇ⁷   B⁷ Bᵇ⁷ Eᵇ-

(B) | **Co** | **Fo** | **Co** | **Fo** | **Aᵇd** **GᵇΔ⁷⁹** | **Gᵇd Fo** |
  Co⁷ F⁷ Bᵇ⁷ Co⁷ F⁷ Bᵇ⁷ Aᵇ-7 Dᵇ⁷ GᵇΔ⁷ \ B⁷ Bᵇ⁷

| **Bᵇd Aᵇd** | **Gᵇd Fo** |
  Eᵇ⁷ Dᵇ⁷ B⁷ Bᵇ⁷

Observe that in the first bar of (A), we use only one scale over two chords which are very similar. In fact, $Eᵇ{-}^6 = Co^7$, or generally, $^bIII{-}^6 = Io^7$:

$Eᵇ{-}^6$:	Eᵇ	Gᵇ		Bᵇ	C
	1	ᵇ3		5	6
Co^7:	Eᵇ	Gᵇ		Bᵇ	C
	ᵇ3	ᵇ5		7	1
Eᵇd:	Eᵇ	Gᵇ	Aᵇ	Bᵇ	C

The last 2 bars of (A) (1ˢᵗ ending), **B⁷** – **Bᵇ⁷**, together with the first, **Eᵇ-/Co⁷**, are an example of the **I-⁽⁷⁾** – **ᵇVI⁷ (- V⁷)** progression (see p. 137 ff), with **I** = **Eᵇ**, and the reversed order (**B⁷** – **Bᵇ⁷** – **Eᵇ-**). A variation of this progression with **I⁷** instead of **I-⁷**, **I⁷** – **ᵇVII⁷** – **ᵇVI⁷** – **V⁷**, is formed by the last 2 bars of (B) (again **I** = **Eᵇ**). Still another progression of that sort is hidden in bars 4 and 5 of (A), **(ᵇIII-⁷)** – **ᵇVI⁷** – **(II-⁷)** – **V⁷** – **I-⁷**, with **I** = **Aᵇ**.

Improvisation on ballads is a difficult task and a challenge. Although the tempo is slow, the changes are rather fast, often half-bar- or sometimes even, like in this case, quarter-bar-wise. Moreover, they ask for a vertical rather than a horizontal approach, if you want to match their colours and moods.

Freedom Jazz Dance

A 'One-Chord-Tune', the chord is supposed to be **Bᵇ⁷**. Many Funk tunes are of the same structure, usually a bass line mainly using root, 5ᵗʰ, 7ᵗʰ, and the octave supports the improviser. In the case of **Freedom Jazz Dance** the theme mostly consists of **4ᵗʰ-chord arpeggios**, starting with notes of the **Bᵇ-Blues-Pentatonic.** In practice, the underlying chord should theoretically be **Bᵇ⁴⁷**, as there is much emphasis on the 11 in the theme, a 'problematic' note over **Bᵇ⁷**. So, from now on, **we will suppose the underlying chord to be Bᵇ⁴⁷** (or one of the possible substitutions for it).

Before talking about options for the improvisation, I would like to **analyse the theme** shortly, relating the tonal material to Bᵇ⁷. It consists of **3 phrases**, which I relate here **in terms of the Bᵇ⁷-chord notes:**

1) <u>5 1 11</u> 13 <u>9 5 3</u> <u>1 5 11</u> <u>1 11</u> <u>7 #9</u> 1

2) <u>1 5 9</u> #9 <u>1 11</u> 9 <u>#9 7 11</u> <u>1 5</u>

3) <u>11 7 5 1 11</u> #9 #5 b9 b5 3 Δ7 9 13 1 b9 b5 #9 9 5 1 5

<u>11 7 #9 #5</u> 13 9 1 7 1 1

The lines under the numbers indicate the **4th-chord arpeggios**, which are successively (the complete chords, or part of them):

1) F^{47}, C^{47}, F^{47}, B^{b47}, A^{b47}

2) C^{47}, B^{b47}, $E^{b47}+F^{47}$

3) E^{b47}, F^{47}, $F^{\#47}$, E^{47}, D^{47}, D^{b47}, C^{47}, $E^{b47}+D^{b47}$

All of the **4th-chord arpeggios** of the first 2 phrases, plus the first 2 of the 3rd, **tonally belong to $B^{b}p(9)$,** as you can easily see. **With the next 2 chords ($F^{\#47}$ and E^{47}), we move a h.s. upwards to Bp(9),** to which these chords belong. **Bp(9)** is as follows:

Bp(9):   **B**   **C#**   **D**   **E**   **F#**   **A**

This, written in terms of chord notes of B^{b7}, becomes the scale:

Bp(9):   **b9**   **#9**   **3**   **b5**   **#5**   **Δ7**

It consists mostly of the altered notes of B^{b7}. Indeed, if we chose **G#** instead of **A**, we would move in **Bd(9)**, which is the altered scale of B^{b7}, **Bmmi,** short of one note, the chord root **B^{b}**. This is the better choice of scale, in my opinion, as it contains the chord note **7** instead of the 'alien' **Δ7**; which, as part of E^{47}, actually occurs in the theme here. However, it occurs at a point very carefully chosen, falls on an offbeat, and is part of a row of quickly changing arpeggios. The theme is no doubt a great and daring piece of music.

There follows a **chromatic descent of 4th-arpeggios, D^{47}, D^{b47}, and C^{47},** which amounts to an oscillation between non-altered **(9, 13)**, altered **(b9**

Examples
_____

b5 #9), and once more non-altered (**9 5 1 5**) notes. This oscillation is continued with the non-altered (**11, 7**) notes of E^{b47} and the altered ones (**#9, #5**) of D^{b47}, ending up with straight non-altered notes.

Often this kind of using different 4th-chord-arpeggios, or, more generally, pentatonics, is called '**outside playing**'. If we look carefully however, we realize that in a way we're **always 'inside'; either inside the pentatonic belonging to B^{b47}, or in its altered scale.**

Sequels of 4th-chord-arpeggios are a bit difficult to play on most instruments, as they consist of rather big intervals, but it is worth practising them. They sound 'abstract' in a way, and enrich the musical vocabulary. I suggest to start practising the chords inside the hexatonic **$B^{b}p(9)$**, those with their roots inside the pentatonic a w.s. higher, **Cp**:

	C^{47}	E^{b47}	F^{47}	G^{47}	B^{b47}	C^{47}
$B^{b}p$:	B^b	D^b	E^b	F	A^b	B^b
(Fp ⊂ $B^b p(9)$)	F	A^b	B^b	C	E^b	F
Cp:	C	E^b	F	G	B^b	C

If you want to add 'outside' 4th-chords, try some of these:

	C^{47}	D^{b47}	E^{b47}	F^{47}	G^{47}	A^{b47}	B^{b47}
		B^b	**B**	D^b	E^b	F	G^b	A^b
		F	G^b	A^b	B^b	C	D^b	E^b
A^bmma:	C	D^b	E^b	F	G	A^b	B^b

We **embed Cp in A^bmma** and use all of the 4th-chords with their roots in that scale. This gives the **additional 4th-chords D^{b47} and A^{b47}**, which consist completely (**D^{b47}: #9, #5, b9**) or partly (**A^{b47}: 7, #9, #5**) of altered notes. We could make use of D^{47} **(3, 13, 9)** and G^{b47} **(#5, b9, b5)**, too (as the freedom jazz dance theme actually does). I leave the use of the last 3 4th-chords of the chromatic scale, E^{47}, A^{47}, and B^{47}, to your taste and preference. They all contain a 'problematic note', **A**, the alteration of a crucial chord note, the **7**, into **Δ7** (though one of them, E^{47}, is used in the jazz dance theme, as we saw above).

Let's now state a **rule**, rather simple to memorize:

On the chord I^7 you can use the arpeggios of the 4th-chords whose roots lie in ^bVIImma, the mma-scale with its root a w.s. lower.

(In our case, the chord is B^{b7}, and the roots of the chord arpeggios lie in **A^bmma**.)

As for the scales that can be used on this tune, you are free to make use of everything we discussed in chapter 7, which was quite a lot.

I find it to be a general rule not only in music, but in many aspects of life, that if the freedom of choice is too big, it rather prevents you from choosing. For this reason, I would like to discuss some possible concepts of how to approach this task.

There is a certain monotony in the accompaniment, if there is just one basic chord and a few basic notes in the bass line. You, as an improviser, should break this monotony, which is just meant to provide you with a lot of freedom. Use this freedom by playing harmonic progressions over this monotonous background. You can play anything you would play on the **II-V-I progression** of which B^{b7} is the **V**, for example, **Fp – Fo(7) – $E^b Δ^{79}$** (see also chapter 9). By doing so, we generally move inside **(1) E^bmma** or, B^b mixolydic, as the scale theorists would call it in this situation.

Another option would be to interpret B^{b47} as B^{b-7}, the **III** of **(2) G^bmma**, and play this scale alternating with **Fo(7)** (which is just one note, G^b, short **of E^bhmi**). This provides a certain 'spanish' flavour. Now, having these two options, try to use both of them even within a single phrase, switching smoothly from one to the other. If you also add the use of the diminished scale **Bdim**, the altered scale **Bmmi**, as well as its 'tritone partner', **Fmmi**, then you have enough material to relate a 'never ending musical story'. That should give you at least enough to have something interesting to say for more than 16 bars...

Yet another idea is instead of using 4ᵗʰ-chord-arpeggios, to also use arpeggios of major or minor triads. But which of the 12 that we have in store fit the chord? If we agree on the use of all 12 notes of the chromatic scale, except the Δ7 of B♭ (A), then we rule out all triads which contain it, the **A-, F-, and D-major triads** and the **A-, G♭-, and D-minor triads.** We would then be left with these chord sequences:

maj triads: **A♭**   **B♭**   **B**   **C**   **D♭**   **E♭**   **E**   **G♭**   **G**

min triads: **A♭**   **B♭**   **B**   **C**   **D♭**   **E♭**   **E**   **F**   **G**

The result would be that you could use all arpeggios of the triads from this list, which is, of course, impossible to memorize for practical purposes. Although, those two nine-tone-scales both contain several cnc-scales. The first one contains both **Bmma** and **Bhma,** the second even all of **A♭mma/i/hma/i.** So, one rather easy to memorize rule, could be:

Improvising on Bᵇ⁷ we can make use of arpeggios of the maj triads with their roots in Bmma, and of the min triads with their roots in A♭mma.

These two rows of maj and min triads, **Bmma** and **A♭mma**, are both closely connected with the two mma-scales we suggested above, **(1)** **E♭mma** and **(2) G♭mma.**

Indeed, taking a closer look at those two scales (representing **Bmma** a bit differently than usual, with flats instead of sharps):

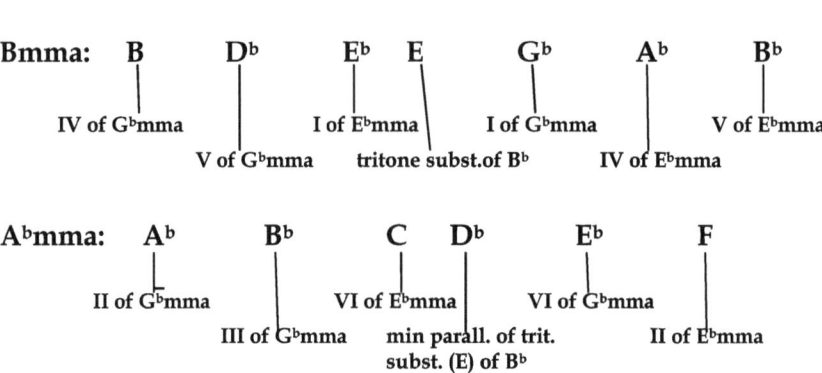

We see that 6 of the 7 **maj triads** with their roots in **Bmma** are just those maj triads which form the **I, IV,** and **V** of the two scales **E♭mma** and **G♭mma**. The 7th, **E**, when completed to **E⁷**, is the tritone substitution of **B♭⁷**.

Likewise, 6 of the 7 **min triads** with their roots in **A♭mma** are the min triads which form the **II, III,** and **VI** of the same two scales **E♭mma** and **G♭mma**.

Thus, using these maj and min triad arpeggios, we basically move inside the two scales **E♭mma** and **G♭mma**. In a way we oscillate between them, producing an effect to the ear that is sometimes called 'outside playing'. As I already mentioned, in my opinion there is no real 'outside playing', except when you use notes at random, which does not make much sense in a harmonic structure. Everything else you do that sounds 'outside' and cool at the same time will have some logical connection to the underlying harmonic structure, no matter how remote and far-fetched it may seem.

To generalize these results, we state as a general rule:

Improvising on I⁷ we can make use of arpeggios of the maj triads with their roots in ♭IImma, and of the min triads with their roots in ♭VIImma.

These are just a few ideas to get you started. I suggest you study the tonal material of chapter 7 and create your own personal ideas.

Dolphin Dance

Chord Progression

	: C-⁷	Ab∅⁷	C-⁷	A-⁷ D⁷	GΔ⁷	Ab-⁷ Db⁷
F-⁷	Bb⁷	C-⁷	C-⁷/Bb	A-⁷	D⁷	GΔ⁷
F/G	A/G	F/G	Eb/F	D/F	Eb/F	E-⁷ A⁷
Eb∅⁷	A-⁷ D⁷	B-⁷	E⁷ D-⁷	C#-⁷	F#⁷	B-⁷
A-⁷/B	B-⁷	A-⁷/B		Bb-⁷	EbΔ⁷	Bb47*
Do⁷ G⁷ :	

Scale Progression

	: Cp	Ao(7)	Cp	Ao(7)	GΔ⁷⁹	Abd	Fp
Fo(7)	Cp	%	Ap	Ao(7)	GΔ⁷⁹	Cmma
Dmmi	Cmma	Bbmma	Cmmi	Bbmma	Eo(7)
%	Ao(7)	Bp	Bo(7)	Dbp	Dbo(7)	Bp(9)
Bp(b9)	Bp(9)	Bp(b9)		Cp(b9)	Cp(9)	Cp(b9)
Do(7) :	

Following the logical structure of the tune, a chorus should start with the last 4 chords after the double bar-line and end with the chords before the double bar-line.

In **bar 2 (Ab7)** we would rather expect to find the scale **Ebo(7)**; however, to my ears, **Ao(7)** (belonging to **D7**, the tritone substitution of **Ab7**) sounds better in the context. Note that it simultaneously contains **Gb** and **G**, the 7 and the Δ⁷ of the chord, as does the 'Coltrane scale' **Bbdim.**

*This is a reharmonization, the original has EoΔ⁷.

A similar situation occurs in **bar 21**. The chord here, **E♭7**, is the tritone substitution of the previous chord, **A7**. It seems more logical to continue with **Eo(7)** on it than to change to another scale more closely related to **E♭7**. The transition to the following scale, **Ao(7)**, is familiar to the ear as it is employed in many other situations. This is a good example of how the harmonic neighborhood of a chord influences the choice of scales.

Bars 14-16 and 17-19:

The scales here (**Cmma** and **Dmmi,** resp. **Bbmma** and **Cmmi**) only differ by one note. So, it might be a good strategy to use chord arpeggios and pentatonics they have in common, such as **Dd** instead of **Cmma** and **Dmmi.**

Bars 30-32 (after the double bar-line):

The chords **B♭-7** and **E♭Δ7** are not incorporated together in any of our cnc-scales. They are however connected by the pentatonic scale **Cp.** In app. 5 (p. 233) you find the two equations 7) **Ip(♭9) = ♭VIId(9)** and 8) **Ip(9) = ♭VIImd(9).**

In our case, 7) **Cp(♭9) = B♭d(9)** and 8) **Cp(9) = B♭md(9)** .

Equation 7) tells us that **Cp(♭9)** is a good interpretation of **B♭-7**. **B♭md** can be interpreted as **E♭Δ79**; thus, equation 8) tells us the same for **Cp(9)** and **E♭Δ79**.

Blue Bossa

Chord Progression

$$|| \text{ C- } | \% | \text{ F- } | \% | \text{Do}^7 | \text{G}^7 | \text{ C- } | \% | \text{E♭-}^7 |$$
$$|\text{A♭}^7| \text{ D♭}\Delta^7 | \% | \text{Do}^7 | \text{G}^7 | \text{ C- } | \text{Do}^7 \text{ G}^7 ||$$

Examples

Bars 1 through 8 and 13 through 16 are harmonically like a C minor Blues, **I (C-)**, **IV (F-)**, and **V (G^7** preceded by the **II, Do^7)**. The interesting part is the maj II-V-I progression in bars 9 through 12, especially the transition from **D^{b}Δ^7** to **Do^7** (see app. 5, p. 178).

Scale Progression

**| | Cd | % | Do(7) | % | % | A^{b}mmi | Cd | % |
|E^{b}p| E^{b}o(7) | A^{b}md(Δ^7)** (= D^{b}Δ$^{79\#11}$) **| % | Do(7) |
|% | Cd | Do(7) | |**

The Δ^7 of **A^{b}md** in bar 11 (the $^{\#}11$ of **D^{b}Δ^7**) is optional.

Epistrophy

This tune is a challenge for improvisers, as the A-part consists of half-bar oszillations between two pairs of 7th-chords with their roots a h.s. apart (**C$^{\#7*}$ – D^7** and **E^{b7} – E^7**).

Such a pair of 7th-chords is nothing new for us in itself. See our discussion of the chord progression **I-^{7} – ^{b}VII^7 – ^{b}VI^7 – V^7** on page 8 above. There, I suggested the use of **Bo(7)** over both **E^7** and **F^7** in a quickly changing progression of these two chords (generally, **Vo(7)** over **I^7** and **^{b}II^7**).

It was a compromise, and **Vo(7)** is an eigenscale of **I^7**, but definitely not of **^{b}II^7**. As a check of the list at the end of chapter 6 (p. 81, under 5)) reveals, there is only one candidate under the eigenscales of **I^7** that could be considered an eigenscale of **^{b}II^7** too, the diminished scale **VIIdim****. Indeed, making the transition **I' = ^{b}II,** we obtain **VII = ^{b}VII'**; which shows

---

* We will interpret **C$^{\#7}$** as the Dominant 7th of **F$^{\#}$hmi** in this context. This denotation of the chord is preferable to **D^{b7}**, as **F$^{\#}$hmi** contains only sharps.
As we saw (see the discussion in chapter 6 under 5), p. 60), this scale (we called it 'Coltrane scale') is not even a genuine eigenscale of **I^7, because the root I is not part of it.

us that this scale is simultaneously the **VIIdim** of I^7 and the **ᵇVII'dim** of $I'^7 = {}^\flat II^7$. This means we can use it in improvisation over both chords. In this example, we can use **Cdim** over $C^{\#7}$ and D^7 and **Ddim** over $E^{\flat7}$ and E^7.

However, there are more possibilities. As I already mentioned, the eigenscales are not the only possible choices for improvisers. In this case, let's see what emerges if we put the two chords together (choosing the pair $C^{\#7} - D^7$ as an example):

$C^{\#7}$:	C#		E#		G#		B	
D^7:		D		F#		A		C
	C#	D	E#	F#	G#	A	B	C

We see that the result is not a cnc-scale, as it contains the 3 consecutive h.s. **B-C- C#-D.** The sequence **E# - F# - G# - A,** two h.s. separated by a w.s. (a typical feature of the mmi- and hmi-scales) suggests that one should try using **F#** as a root. The scale then becomes:

F#hmi(#11): F#   G#   A   B (C) C#   D   E#

Observe that this scale contains our familiar **G#o(7)-** hexatonic, a very frequent choice for the chord $C^{\#7}$. If you exchange **C#** for **C** in this scale, then you get **G#obl(7),** which is also contained in **F#hmi(#11).**

G#o(7): G#   B   C# D   E# F#

G#obl(7): G#   B C   D   E# F#

At the same time, **G#obl(7)** is part of **Cdim,** the common eigenscale of both $C^{\#7}$ and D^7. Consequently, these results suggest to use this hexatonic in this situation. This tune provides us at last with a good example for the use of this scale. As **G#o(7)** is the better choice for $C^{\#7}$, you can take the challenge, if you like, and try to oscillate between these 2 scales which differ only in one note (**C** vs. **C#**), half-bar-wise.

Examples

Another scale that works well here is one closely related with **F#hmi(#11)**, **Ahma(#9)**.

Ahma(#9):   A   B (C)   C#   D   E   F   G#,

A hexatonic contained in it, **Bo(7)**, works here as well.

We are provided with yet another scale if we exchange the D in **F#hmi(#11)** for **D#**. Indeed, **D#** works well with both **C#7** and **D7**, being the **9** of the one and the **b9** of the other. Making this exchange, we land inside the scale:

F#mmi(#11):   F#   G#   A   B (C)   C#   D#   E#

Omitting the root, **F#** (the 'problematic note' **11** over **C#7**), we are left with the hexatonic **G#d(b9)**; which, in my opinion, sounds especially good in this situation, using the **C** as an occasional additional note.

To sum up our results, over the two chords **C#7** and **D7**, we can alternatively use the scales **G#obl(7)** (**F#hmi(#11)** or **Cdim**), **Bo(7)** (**Ahma(#9)**), or **G#d(b9)** (**F#mmi(#11)**). In general, over the two chords **I7** and **bII7**, we can alternatively use the scales **Vobl(7)** (**IVhmi(#11)** or **VIIdim**), **bVIIo(7)** (**bVIhma(#9)**), or **Vd(b9)** (**IVmmi(#11)**).

Observe that none of these suggested scales are eigenscales of both of these chords. They all sound interesting if played over them, as they are made up of several altered chord extensions of the two chords. The following two tables (containing the hexatonics) show how:

I7:	I				III		V		bVII	
	b9				3	4	5		7	Δ7
Vobl(7):	bII				III	IV	V		bVII	VII
	b9		#9		3		5		7	
bVIIo(7):	bII		bIII		III		V	bVI	bVII	
	root	9			3		5	b13	7	
Vd(b9):	I	II			III		V	bVI	bVII	

	C0	C1	C2	C3	C4	C5	C6	C7	C8	C9
♭II⁷:		♭II				IV		♭VI		VII
		root			♯9	3	♯11		13	7
Vobl(7):		♭II		III		IV	V		♭VII	VII
		root		9	♯9		♯11	5	13	
♭VIIo(7):		♭II	♭III	III			V	♭VI	♭VII	
	Δ7		♭9		♯9		♯11	5	13	
Vd(♭9):	I	II		III			V	♭VI	♭VII	

There are two places in these scales where the normally 'problematic' note Δ7 (when played over a 7th-chord) shows up, in **Vobl(7)** over I⁷ and in **Vd(♭9)** over ♭II⁷. In **Vobl(7)**, part of the 'Coltrane scale' **VIIdim**, both 7 and Δ7 are present. This is not the case in **Vd(♭9)**. Yet, in the context, both scales sound consistent and logical, at least to my ears. Of course, it all depends on the nature of the phrases you want to play. If you feel like hammering staccato 16th notes for a while, perhaps you'd better use some other note than the Δ7.

The B-part of the tune is comparably straightforward. This is the complete chord progression:

```
|| C#7 D7 | % | % | % | Eb7 E7 | % | % | % | % |
| % | % | % | C#7 D7 | % | % | % || F#- | % |
| % | % | B7 | % | C#7 | D7 || Eb7 E7 | % | % |
| % | C#7 D7 | % | % | % ||
```

Examples

Thus, a corresponding scale progression could be:

	G#obl(7)/Bo(7)/G#d(♭9)	%	%	%
B♭obl(7)/D♭o(7)/B♭d(♭9)	%	%	%
%	%	%	%	G#obl(7)/Bo(7)/G#d(♭9)	%
%	% || F#d	%	%	%	%	% |G#d
Ad		B♭obl(7)/D♭o(7)/B♭d(♭9)	%	%	%
G#obl(7)/Bo(7)/G#d(♭9)	%	%	%	

One last remark:

If you are not especially fond of the sound of the obl(7)-scales, you can replace them by their o(7)-namesakes in the above progression.

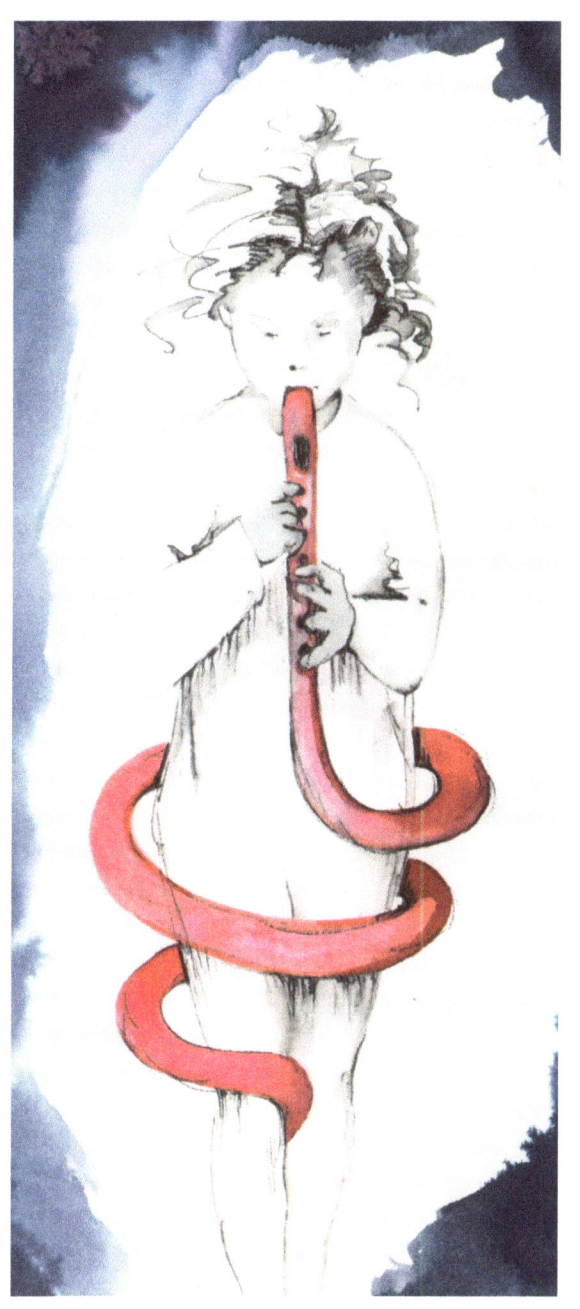

App. 1: Pentatonics and CNC-Scales

Here is a list of the pentatonic-types from chapter 5 contained in each cnc-scale.

scales	pentatonics contained							
Imma	Imd	IIp/d	IIIp		Vmd		VIp	
Immi	Id	IIp/d						
Ihmi		IIo				ᵇVIobl		VIIobl
Ihma		IIo			Vmd	ᵇVIobl		VIIo
Idim	Io	IIobl	ᵇIIIo	IVobl	ᵇVo	ᵇVIobl	VIo	VIIobl
Iaug(wt)		none						
Iaug(hta)		none						

App. 2: Intervals and Chord Notation

The most straightforward way to define the intervals of our 12-tone-system is to shape them on the scale degree notation. Remember that this notation itself was shaped on the set of the (melodic) major scale

I II III IV V VI VII.

The first step is to define the **interval of a 2nd as the pair of notes I – II**, that of **a 3rd as the pair of notes I – III**, etc. Next, we call these intervals more precisely **maj 2nd, maj 3rd, perf 4th, perf 5th, maj 6th, and maj 7th**. The intervals between I and the rest of the notes of our 12-tone-system I - ♭II, I – ♭III, I – #IV (I – ♭V), I – ♭VI, I –♭VII, we call **min 2nd, min 3rd, aug 4th (dim 5th), min 6th, and (min) 7th**.

We define the interval of a **perf 8th**, or **octave**, as the pair of notes I – I', where I' is physically the tone with the double frequency of that of I. The higher intervals of **min** and **maj 9th, min** and **maj 10th**, ... are the pairs of notes I – ♭II', I – II', I – ♭III', I – III', ...etc. Moreover, it is convenient to define the interval **aug 9th** as the pair of notes I - #II' (= I - ♭III'), as it simplifies matters when we are dealing with chords like $I^{7\#9}$ (see chapter 7, p. 88).

These definitions are in accordance with general tradition, which has proved to be very useful in the course of time, and also coincide with our definitions from chapter 3.

With these interval definitions, we are now ready to define the eigenchords of our cnc-scales in a more general fashion. Here we do not restrict ourselves to the examination of tetrachords; the chords may contain more notes, but the construction rule is the same as in chapter 4. That is, our chords are supposed to be of the 'strict' form

X X+2 X+4 X+6 X+8 ...,

where X is any note of a cnc-scale and 2, 4, 6, ... are the numbers of steps from this note inside the scale. For example, if **X = G** in the scale **Fmmi**, we get the multi-note-chord:

G B♭ D F A♭ C ...

It is immediately clear that 'multi-note-chord' is a bit of an exaggeration. No eigenchord of a cnc-scale can contain more than the 6, 7, or 8 different notes the scale contains (except for octave duplication). Thus, the largest eigenchord of **Fmma** with root **G** is:

$$\textbf{G B}^\flat \textbf{ D F A}^\flat \textbf{ C E}$$

Or, in its abstract form:

$$\textbf{X X+2 X+4 X+6 X+8 X+10 X+12}$$

The first part of the multichord above, **G B**$^\flat$ **D F**, forms the chord **G-7**, with intervals **root, (min)3rd, (perf)5th, (min)7th**. For the last 3 notes, **A$^\flat$, C**, and **E**, it seems reasonable to call them the **9th, 11th**, and **13th** of the chord. To be more exact, we call **A$^\flat$** the $^\flat$**9** of **G-7**, as **G-A$^\flat$** form a h.s. (the **9** would be **A**); the corresponding interval is a **(min) 2nd**. Accordingly, **C** is called the chord's **11;** the corresponding interval being a **(perf) 4th**. Finally, **E** is called the chord's **13**, and the name of the corresponding interval is a **(maj) 6th**.

In the light of this example, it seems reasonable to give all 12 scale degrees the following note names, seen as parts of a chord with root I:

scale degree:	I	$^\flat$II	II	$^\flat$III	III	IV	#IV	V	$^\flat$VI	VI	$^\flat$VII	VII
note name:	root	$^\flat$9	9	$^\flat$3/#9	3	4/11	#11/$^\flat$5	5	#5/$^\flat$13	13	7	Δ7

The 12 tetrachords we listed in chapter 3 all consisted of the **root**, the $^\flat$**3** or **3**, the $^\flat$**5, 5** or #**5**, and the **7** or Δ**7**; the two triads 13) and 14) of the **root**, the **4**, and the **7** or Δ**7**. The additional notes of our eigen-multichords, $^\flat$**9, 9, #9, 11, #11, $^\flat$13**, and **13**, we will call **chord extensions**. They will be part of the name of the chords they belong to. For example, the chord mentioned above is called **G-7$^{\flat 9/11/13}$**.

Take notice that as the diminished and augmented scales contain an even number of notes (**8** and **6**), their strict eigen-multichords contain no more than the **4** and **3** notes that constitute our already known tetrachords (triads). For example, in **Iaug(hta)** the formula **X X+2 X+4 ... X+12** yields, for **X = I, I III $^\flat$VI I III $^\flat$VI I = I III $^\flat$VI = I+.**

App. 3: Complete List of Triads

The chord progressions of most pieces of music that you will come across are made up of triads and tetrachords. Pentachords and even bigger chords may also occur, but usually they can be replaced by 'thinned-out' tetrachord versions of themselves without losing any essential notes.

In any case, it would be convenient to have complete lists of all the chords you might have to deal with. Here, and in appendix 4, I provide you with the two lists of all possible triads and tetrachords in our 12-tone-system that respond to rule 1 of chapter 2 (they do not contain any two consecutive h.s.). We are not so much interested in partially chromatic chords here, as they cannot be eigenchords of our cnc-scales.

All existent chords of that form can be interpreted, from a formal mathematical/ combinatorial point of view, as versions of the **12 tetrachords, the triads 13) and 14)** of chapter 3, plus the 5 basic triads **Io (dim triad, I-^{b}III-^{b}V), I- (min triad, I-^{b}III-V), I (maj triad, I-III-V), I+ (aug triad, I-III-$^\#$V), and IØ (half-dim triad, I-III-^{b}V).**

- What do I exactly mean by 'versions' of chords?

I would like to define the **version of a chord** as either the **unchanged chord itself,** or the **chord without its 3rd or 5th,** and another additional note (usually one of the **'chord extensions'** ^{b}9, 9, $^\#$9, 11, $^\#$11, ^{b}13, or 13; see appendix 2). The chord **X without its 3rd** is denoted as **X\3, without its 5th as X\5.**

We discussed earlier (see chap. 6, p. 61), that in a voicing of I^7 we can leave out the **5th (I^7\5),** without essentially changing the chord quality. The same holds true for **all chords with a perfect 5th,** that is, for the **triads I- and I,** as well as for the **tetrachords I-^{7}, I-Δ^7, I^7, and IΔ^7.**

On the contrary, if we leave out the 3rd of a chord instead, this will affect the chord quality quite a lot. In fact, the result is an 'open sounding' chord, in the sense that it is neither major nor minor.

Now, let's take a look at the list of triads:

List of Triads

	rel.int.st.*	triads							chord name
1)	1 2 9:	I	ᵇII	ᵇIII					I-ᵇ9\5
2)	1 3 8:	I	ᵇII		III				Iᵇ9\5; ᵇII-Δ7\5
3)	1 4 7:	I	ᵇII		IV				ᵇIIΔ7\5
4)	1 5 6:	I	ᵇII			ᵇV			IØᵇ9\3; ᵇII4Δ7; ᵇV#11\3
5)	1 6 5:	I	ᵇII			V			Iᵇ9\3; ᵇIIφΔ7\3
6)	1 7 4:	I	ᵇII				ᵇVI		I+ᵇ9\3; ᵇIIΔ7\3; ᵇVI11\5
7)	1 8 3:	I	ᵇII				VI		ᵇII+Δ7\3; VI#9\5
8)	1 9 2:	I	ᵇII					ᵇVII	ᵇVII-9\5
9)	2 2 8:	I	II	III					I9\5; III+7\5
10)	2 3 7:	I	II		IV				II-7\5
11)	2 4 6:	I	II			ᵇV			IØ9\3; II7\5; ᵇV+#11\3
12)	2 5 5:	I	II			V			I9\3; II47; V11\3
13)	2 6 4:	I	II				ᵇVI		I+9\3; ᵇVIØ; IIφ7\3
14)	2 7 3:	I	II				VI		II7\3
15)	3 3 6:	I		ᵇIII		ᵇV			Io
16)	3 4 5:	I		ᵇIII		V			I-; V+11\3
17)	3 5 4:	I		ᵇIII			ᵇVI		I+#9\3; ᵇVI (maj triad)
18)	4 4 4:	I		III			ᵇVI		I/III/ᵇVI+

Indeed, studying the column of chord names, we see that all chords can be interpreted as versions of the 19 (14 plus 5) chords mentioned above; often in more than one possible way.

*relative interval structure. The numbers are the numbers of h.s. between the chord notes. For example, in the first line 129 means we have **1 h.s.** between I and ᵇII, **2** between ᵇII and ᵇIII, and **9** between ᵇIII and I.

App. 4: Complete List Of Tetrachords

In appendix 3, we defined the **version of a chord** to be either the **unchanged chord** itself, or the **chord without its 3rd or 5th, with another note added instead** (usually one of the 'chord extensions' $^{b}9$, 9, $^{#}9$, 11, $^{#}11$, $^{b}13$, or 13; see p. 168). In the following list, we also need the concept of '**extended versions' of triads.** An extended version of a triad is the tetrachord consisting of the complete triad and a chord extension. For example, under **4)** we find the **extended version I-^{b9} of I-.** The chord X without its 3rd will be denoted as X\3, without its 5th as X\5.

List of Tetrachords

rel.int.st.*				tetrachords							chord name
1) 1218	I	^{b}II	^{b}III	III							^{b}II-Δ^{79}\5; III+$\Delta^{7/13}$\3
2) 1227	I	^{b}II	^{b}III		IV						^{b}IIΔ^{79}\5
3) 1236	I	^{b}II	^{b}III			^{b}V					Io^{b9}; ^{b}II$^{4}\Delta^{79}$; ^{b}III-$^{7/13}$\5
4) 1245	I	^{b}II	^{b}III				V				I-^{b9}; ^{b}III$^{7/13}$\5; ^{b}IIØΔ^{79}\3
5) 1254	I	^{b}II	^{b}III					^{b}VI			^{b}IIΔ^{79}\3; I^{11}
6) 1263	I	^{b}II	^{b}III						VI		^{b}II+Δ^{79}\3; VIØ$^{#9}$; ^{b}III$\phi\Delta^{7/13}$\3
7) 1272	I	^{b}II	^{b}III							^{b}VII	I-^{7b9}\5; ^{b}III$^{7/13}$\3
8) 1317	I	^{b}II		III	IV						^{b}II$\Delta^{7#9}$\5
9) 1326	I	^{b}II		III		^{b}V					IØ^{b9}; ^{b}V$^{7#11}$\3; ^{b}II-$\Delta^{7/11}$\5
10) 1335	I	^{b}II		III			V				^{b}IIoΔ^{7}; I^{b9}
11) 1344	I	^{b}II		III				^{b}VI			^{b}II-Δ^{7}; I+^{b9}; III+^{13}; ^{b}VI+^{11}

*relative interval structure. The numbers are the numbers of h.s. between the chord notes. Take the first line, f.i. : **1218** means we have 1 h.s. between I and ^{b}II, 2 between ^{b}II and ^{b}III, 1 between ^{b}III and III, and 8 between III and I.

rel.int.st.				—tetrachords—							chord name
		I	♭II	II	III	IV	♭V	V	♭VI	VI	♭VII	
12) 1353	I	♭II		III					VI			VI$^{\#9}$
13) 1362	I	♭II		III						♭VII		I^{7b9}\5; ♭VIIo^9; ♭II-Δ$^{7/13}$\5
14) 1416	I	♭II			IV	♭V						♭VΔ$^{7\#11}$\3; ♭IIΔ$^{7/11}$\5
15) 1425	I	♭II			IV		V					♭IIØΔ^7; VØ$^{7/11}$\3
16) 1434	I	♭II			IV			♭VI				♭IIΔ^7
17) 1443	I	♭II			IV				VI			♭II+Δ^7; VI+$^{\#9}$
18) 1452	I	♭II			IV					♭VII		♭IIΔ$^{7/13}$\5; I^{47b9}; ♭VII-^{9}
19) 1515	I	♭II				♭V	V					♭IIØΔ$^{7/11}$\3; VØΔ$^{7/11}$\3
20) 1524	I	♭II				♭V		♭VI				♭II^{45}Δ^7; ♭VI$^{7/11}$\5
21) 1533	I	♭II				♭V			VI			♭V$_{-}^{\#11}$; ♭II+Δ$^{7/11}$\3
22) 1542	I	♭II				♭V				♭VII		♭V$^{\#11}$; IØ^{7b9}\3
23) 1623	I	♭II					V		VI			♭II+Δ$^{7\#11}$\3; VI$^{7\#9}$\5
24) 1632	I	♭II					V			♭VII		I^{7b9}\3; ♭IIØΔ$^{7/13}$\3; Vo^{11}; ♭VII-$^{9/13}$\5
25) 1722	I	♭II						♭VI		♭VII		♭VII-^{79}\5; ♭IIΔ$^{7/13}$\3; I+^{7b9}\3
26) 2226	I		II	III		♭V						II^{79}\5; IØ^9; III+^{79}\3
27) 2235	I		II	III			V					I^9; II^{479}
28) 2244	I		II	III				♭VI				I+^{9}; III+^{7}; ♭VI+$^{\#11}$; IIØ^{79}\3
29) 2253	I		II	III					VI			II^{79}\3; VI-^{11}
30) 2325	I		II		IV		V					V^{457}; II-$^{7/11}$\5
31) 2334	I		II		IV			♭VI				IIo^7; ♭VIØ^{13}
32) 2343	I		II		IV				VI			II-^{7}; IV^6

App. 4: Complete List of Tetrachords

rel.int.st.			tetrachords			chord name
33) **2424**	I	II		$^\flat$V	$^\flat$VI	II∅^{7}; $^\flat$VI∅^{7}
34) **2433**	I	II		$^\flat$V	VI	II^7
35) **3333**	I		$^\flat$III	$^\flat$V	VI	Io

Indeed, studying the column of chord names in this list, we see that all chords can be interpreted as versions of the **12 tetrachords of chap. 3,** or extended versions of the **7 triads X^{47}, X^{4}Δ^7, Xo, X-, X, X+, and X∅**); mostly in more than one possible way.

App. 5: Complete List of Hexatonics

A hexatonic is a combination of 2 triplets of notes that are a h.s. (∩), w.s. (Π), or an a.s. (∧) apart.

As part of a cnc-scale, they must obey rule 1 of chapter 2 (no 2 successive h.s.)
These are the possible triplets, and their symbolic denotation:

triplet	symbol
I—ᵇII————— ᵇIII	A
I————II—ᵇIII	∀
I— ᵇII ————————— III	T
I ————— ᵇIII —ᵇIV	⊥
I —————II ————III	O
I————II—————— IV	E
I ————— ᵇIII ————IV	Ǝ

Here follows the complete list of hexatonics presented as a combination of such triplets. A 4th gap is symbolically represented as Π∩Π, a maj 3rd gap as ΠΠ, while a min 3rd gap is the same as an a.s. (∧).
In the column 'pentatonic interpretation', I have listed the pentatonics of which the hexatonic in question is an extension.

List of Hexatonics

	symbolic presentation	contained in (scales)	pentatonic interpretation

with 4th gap:

| 1) I—ᵇII ——— ᵇIII   III ——— #IV—V | A∩∀∏∩∏ | ᵇIIdim | - |

with maj 3rd gap:

2) I— ᵇII ——— ᵇIII III ——— #IV——#V	A∩O∏∏	ᵇIImmi/ hmi	-
3) I—ᵇII ——— ᵇIII III ———————V–ᵇVI	A∩⊔∏∏	ᵇVIhma	-
4) I— ᵇII ——— ᵇIII IV — ᵇV——ᵇVI	A∏A∏∏	ᵇIImma/ hma	ᵇVImd(7)
5) I— ᵇII ——— ᵇIII IV———————V–ᵇVI	A∏∀∏∏	ᵇVImma	ᵇVImd(Δ7)
6) I— ᵇII ——————III IV———————V–ᵇVI	T∩∀∏∏	IVhmi	-
7) I———————II— ᵇIII IV— ᵇV——ᵇVI	∀∏A∏∏	ᵇIIImmi, Idim	-
8) I ——— II— ᵇIII IV ———————V–ᵇVI	∀∏∀∏∏	ᵇIIImma, Ihmi	-
9) I ——— II———————III IV ———————V–ᵇVI	O∩A∏∏	IVmmi, Ihma	-

with min 3rd gap(s):

10) I— ᵇII ——— ᵇIII ᵇIV——— ᵇV———————VI	A∩E∧	ᵇIIdim/hmi	Iobl(ᵇ9)
11) I—ᵇII ——— ᵇIII ᵇIV———————V———————VI	A∩Ǝ∧	ᵇIIdim ᵇVIIhmi,	-
12) I—ᵇII ——— ᵇIII IV— ᵇV———————VI	A∏T∧	ᵇIIhma	Io(ᵇ9)
13) I—ᵇII ——— ᵇIII IV———————V——— VI	A∏O∧	ᵇVIImmi	Id(ᵇ9)
14) I—ᵇII ——— ᵇIII IV———————#V——— VI	A∏⊔∧	ᵇIIhma	ᵇVImd(ᵇ9) ᵇIII/
15) I—ᵇII ——— ᵇIII #IV—V———————VI	A∧A∧	ᵇIIdim	VIobl(7)
16) I— ᵇII ——— ᵇIII #IV———#V——— VI	A∧∀∧	ᵇIIhma/i	ᵇIIIo(7)
17) I— ᵇII ——————III IV———————#V——— VI	T∩⊔∧	ᵇIIaug(hta)	-
18) I———————II— ᵇIII IV—ᵇV———————VI	∀∏T∧	ᵇVIIhma, Idim	Io(9)
19) I———————II— ᵇIII IV———————V ——— VI	∀∏O∧	ᵇVIImma, Immi	Id(9)

App. 5: Complete List of Hexatonics

(with min 3rd gap(s)):				(symb. presentation	cont. in (scales)	pent. interpr.)
20) I———— II——♭III	IV————————#V——VI			∀Π⌐∧	Idim	-
21) I————II——♭III	#IV————#V——VI			∀∧∀∧	Idim	♭III/
						VIo(Δ⁷)
22) I————II———— III	IV————V————VI			O∩O∧	I/IVmma	Imd(9)
23) I————II———— III	IV————————#V——VI			O∩⌐∧	VIhmi	-
24) I————II———— III	#IV—V————VI			OΠA∧	Vmma/i	VId(7)
25) I————II ———— III	#IV————#V——VI			OΠ∀∧	VImmi	VId(Δ⁷)

no gaps:

26) I———— II———— III	#IV————#V———— #VI			OΠOΠ	Iaug(wt)	-

Here, a list of the important equalities between hexatonics in both directions:

1) Iobl(5) = ♭IIIobl(♭9); Iobl(♭9) = VIobl(5)

2) Iobl(#5) = ♭IIIo(♭9); Io(♭9) = VIobl(#5)

3) Iobl(7) = ♭Vobl(7)

4) Iobl(Δ⁷) = ♭Vo(7); Io(7) = ♭Vobl(Δ⁷)

5) Io(Δ⁷) = ♭Vo(Δ7)

6) Io(9) = VIo(#5); Io(#5) = ♭IIIo(9)

7) Ip(♭9) = ♭VIId(9); Id(9) = IIp(♭9)

8) Ip(9) = Vp(♭13) = ♭VIImd(9); Imd(9) = IIp(9) = VIp(♭13);

   Ip(♭13) = IVp(9) = ♭IIImd(9)

   or, with Imd = IVΔ⁷⁹ (compare p. 42):

   Ip(9) = Vp(♭13) = ♭IIIΔ⁷/⁹/¹³; IVΔ⁷/⁹/¹³ = IIp(9) = VIp(♭13);

   Ip(♭13) = IVp(9) = ♭VIΔ⁷/⁹/¹³

9) Ip(13) = Id(7)

Equations 7 - 9 show that all 4 possible hexatonic extensions of the Blues pentatonic **Ip (Ip(^{b}9), Ip(9), Ip(^{b}13), Ip(13))** can be interpreted in terms of the hexatonic extensions of the other 4 pentatonics we use. That is, on the hexatonic level we do well without the Blues pentatonic, which is unique among the pentatonics of chapter 5, because it contains ^{b}**VII** instead of the **VI** that all the other pentatonics contain.

Not only equations, but also 'inequations' between hexatonics may play an important role in improvisation. For example, compare the two hexatonics **A^{b}md(Δ^7)** and **Do(7)**:

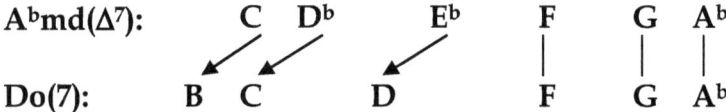

The symbolic representation of **A^{b}md(Δ^7)** is ΑΠⱯ∐∐, that of **Do(7)** is Α∧Ɐ∧ (see the list of hexatonics above, 5) and 16)). They consist of the same form of triplets, **A and Ɐ**. One of the triplets, **Ɐ**, even consists of the same notes (F – G – A^b), while the second, **A**, 'recedes' one h.s. 'backwards' **(C – D^b – E^b** becomes B – C – D). This comparison has indeed a practical use in improvisation. **A^{b}md(Δ^7)** is an interpretation of the chord D^{b}Δ^7, while **Do(7)** is an interpretation of the chord Do^7.

Both chords are contained in the tune Blue Bossa, where we find the sequence of the two II-V-I-progressions (see p. 156):

$$\text{Eb-}^7 - \text{A}^{b7} - \text{D}^b\Delta^7 - \text{Do}^7 - \text{G}^7 - \text{C}$$

I am sure there are many more of these interesting inequations between hexatonics, and I would like to encourage you to look for some. This might be an inspiration for new compositions as well.

Next, I have listed the scales that are generated by the different hexatonics. Generally, as the underlying pentatonics are extended to scales by adding 2 notes (or 3, in the case of the diminished scales), the corresponding 2 (respectively 3) hexatonics generate the same scales.

App. 5: Complete List of Hexatonics

pentatonics	hexatonic extensions	generated scales

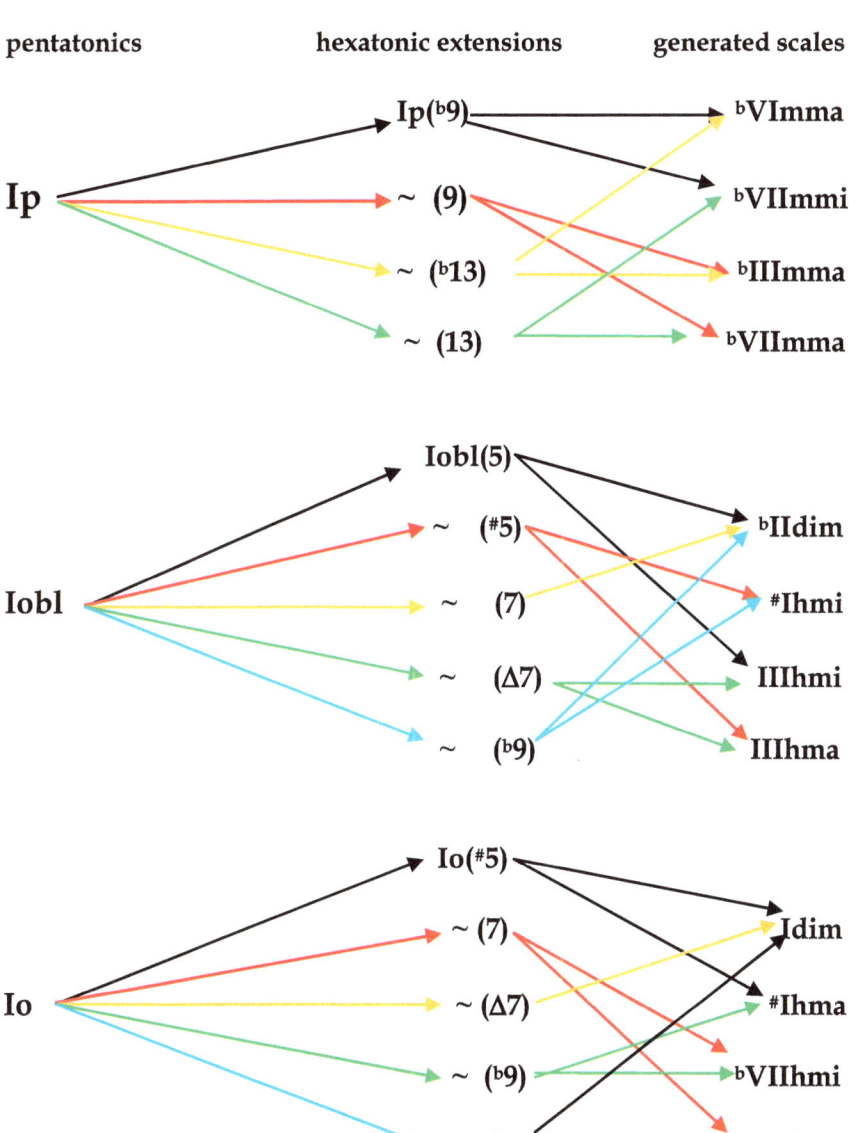

pentatonics	hexatonic extensions	generated scales

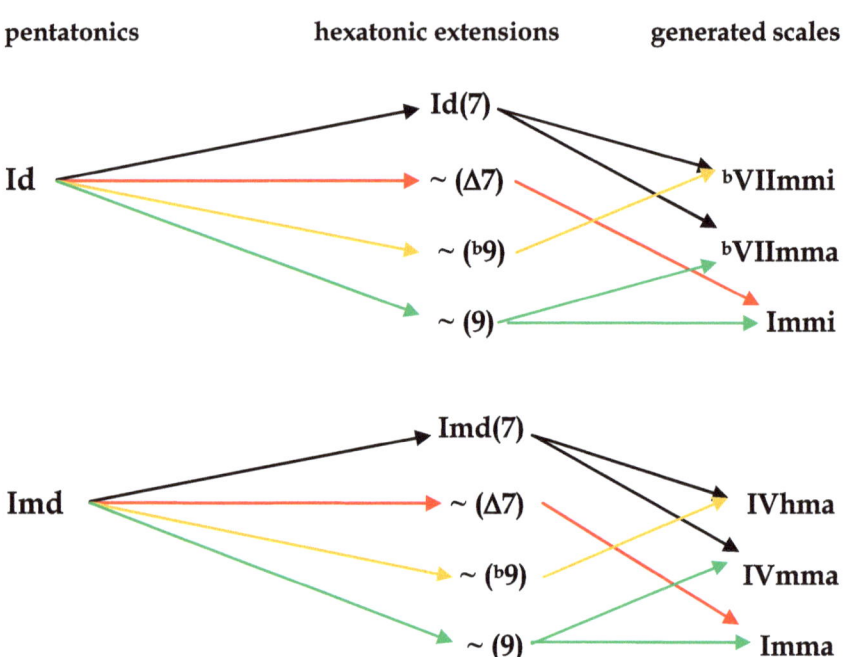

The same relations, more detailed:

	I		II	bIII	IV	V			bVII
Ip:	I			bIII	IV	V			bVII
Ip(b9):		bII							
Ip(b13):							bVI		
bVImma:	I	bII		bIII	IV	V	bVI		bVII
Ip(b9):		bII							
Ip(13):								VI	
bVIImmi:	I	bII		bIII	IV	V		VI	bVII
Ip(9):			II						
Ip(b13):							bVI		
bIIImma:	I		II	bIII	IV	V	bVI		bVII
Ip(9):			II						
Ip(13):								VI	
bVIImmi:	I		II	bIII	IV	V		VI	bVII

App. 5: Complete List of Hexatonics

	I	#VII	♭II / #I	II	♭III / #II	♭IV	III / #III	IV / #IV	♭V	V	#V	VI	♭VII	VII
Iobl:	I				♭III	♭IV			♭V			VI		
Iobl(5):										V				
Iobl(7):													♭VII	
Iobl(♭9):			♭II											
♭IIdim:	I		♭II		♭III	♭IV			♭V	V		VI	♭VII	
Iobl(#5):											#V			
Iobl(♭9):			♭II											
#Ihmi:		#VII	#I		#II		III	#IV			#V	VI		
Iobl(5):										V				
Iobl(Δ7):														VII
IIIhmi:	I				#II		III	#IV		V		VI		VII
Iobl(#5):											#V			
Iobl(Δ7):														VII
IIIhmi:	I				#II		III	#IV			#V	VI		VII
Io:	I				♭III			IV	♭V			VI		
Io(#5):											#V			
Io(Δ7):														VII
Io(9):				II										
Idim:	I			II	♭III			IV	♭V		#V	VI		VII
Io(#5):											#V			
Io(♭9):			♭II											
#Ihma:		#VII	#I		#II		#III	#IV			#V	VI		
Io(7):													♭VII	
Io(♭9):			♭II											
♭VIIhmi:	I		♭II		♭III			IV	♭V			VI	♭VII	
Io(7):													♭VII	
Io(9):				II										
♭VIIhma:	I			II	♭III			IV	♭V			VI	♭VII	

	I	♭II	II	♭III	III	IV	V	VI	♭VII	VII
Id:	I			♭III		IV	V	VI		
Id(7):									♭VII	
Id(♭9):		♭II								
♭VIImmi:	I	♭II		♭III		IV	V	VI	♭VII	
Id(7):									♭VII	
Id(9):			II							
♭VIImma:	I		II	♭III		IV	V	VI	♭VII	
Id(Δ7):										VII
Id(9):			II							
Immi:	I		II	♭III		IV	V	VI		VII
Imd:	I				III	IV	V	VI		
Imd(7):									♭VII	
Imd(♭9):		♭II								
IVhma:	I	♭II			III	IV	V	VI	♭VII	
Imd(7):									♭VII	
Id(9):			II							
IVmma:	I		II		III	IV	V	VI	♭VII	
Imd(Δ7):										VII
Id(9):			II							
Imma:	I		II		III	IV	V	VI		VII

Now, refraining to the most important hexatonics used in improvisation, we obtain the following relations in a **'shortcut list'**, which you will also find in chapter 5:

Shortcut List

pentatonics	hexatonic extensions	generated scales

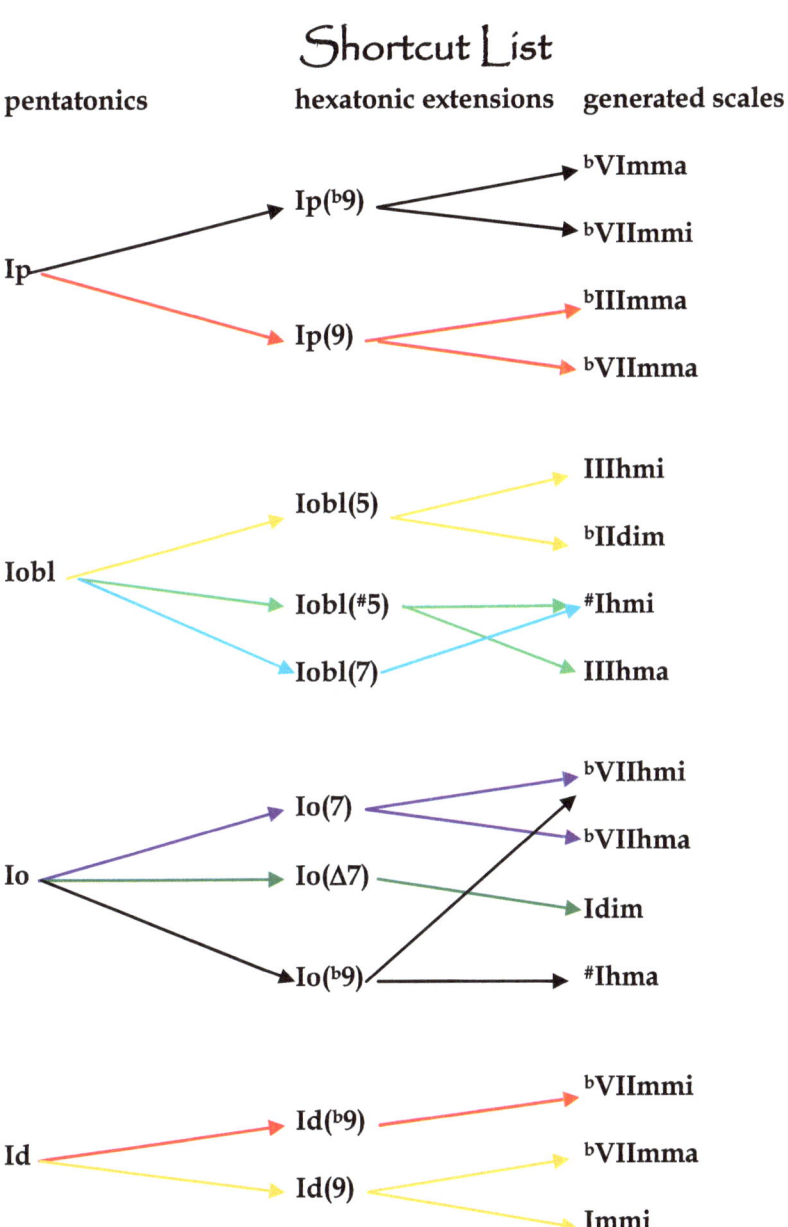

pentatonics

Ip

Iobl

Io

Id

hexatonic extensions

Ip(♭9)

Ip(9)

Iobl(5)

Iobl(♯5)

Iobl(7)

Io(7)

Io(Δ7)

Io(♭9)

Id(♭9)

Id(9)

generated scales

♭VImma

♭VIImmi

♭IIImma

♭VIImma

IIIhmi

♭IIdim

♯Ihmi

IIIhma

♭VIIhmi

♭VIIhma

Idim

♯Ihma

♭VIImmi

♭VIImma

Immi

App. 5: Complete List of Hexatonics

pentatonics   hexatonic extensions   generated scales

                                              IVhma

                          Imd (♭9)

Imd   **Imma**

                          Imd(9)

                                              IVmma

This list could look different, but I chose this presentation for practical reasons. For instance, I could have omitted the hexatonic **Iobl(7)**, because the scale **♭IIdim** is already generated by **Iobl(5)**; however, **Iobl(7)** is easy to learn because of its symmetry (**♭III/VIobl** is of the form **A∧A∧** as we saw), it is also practical to use in some contexts (see 'Epistrophy', p. 157 ff).

App. 6: Scale Relations – Circles of 5ths

It seems natural to consider 2 scales as being related to each other if they differ by only one note. Thus, in the **traditional circle of 5ths** of the **(melodic) major scales,** two neighbouring scales with roots a 5th apart are related (for example, **Fmma** and **B♭mma** differ by the note **E** in **Fmma,** which becomes **E♭** in **B♭mma**).

The situation is somewhat more complicated in the case of the **mmi-,** **hmi-,** and **hma-**scales, as there are no relations between any two scales of the same sort. In other words, each of the **mmi-,** and **hmi-,** and **hma-scales** differ from all of the other scales of the same kind by more than one note. There are however relations between these scales. For example, **Ammi** and **Ahmi** are related, differing by the note **F** in **Ahmi,** which becomes **F#** in **Ammi:**

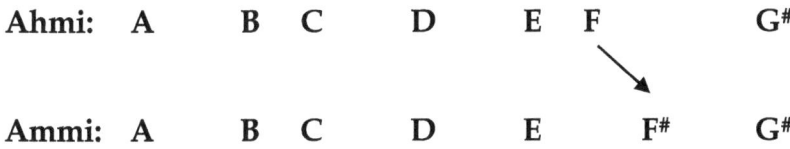

Likewise, **Ammi** and **Ehma** are related – the difference lying in the note **D** of **Ammi,** becoming **D#** in **Ehma:**

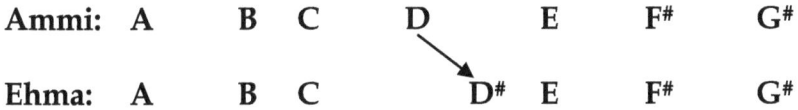

As in the case of the mma-scales, it is possible to construct circles of 5ths for the other scales too, and in more than one conceivable way. In order to do so, let us first study all the possible transitions from one scale to another by changing one note:

App. 6: Scale Relations – Circles of 5ths

1) Imma is related to these scales:

Imma:	I		II			III	IV		V		VI		VII
IImmi:		#I	II			III	IV		V		VI		VII
Immi:	I		II	♭III			IV		V		VI		VII
Vmma:	I		II			III		#IV	V		VI		VII
VIhmi:	I		II			III	IV			#V	VI		VII
Ihma:	I		II			III	IV		V	♭VI			VII
IVmma:	I		II			III	IV		V		VI	♭VII	

2) Immi: Here we have less possibilities. **Immi** can change into **Imma,** **♭VIImma, Ihmi,** and **Vhma**, as is easily verified.

3) Ihmi can change into **♭IIImma, Immi,** and **Ihma.**

4) Ihma can change into **Imma, IVmmi,** and **Ihmi.**

Based on this information, here is a complete **mmi - mma – hma – hmi – 5th circle:**

App. 6: Scale Relations – Circles of 5ths

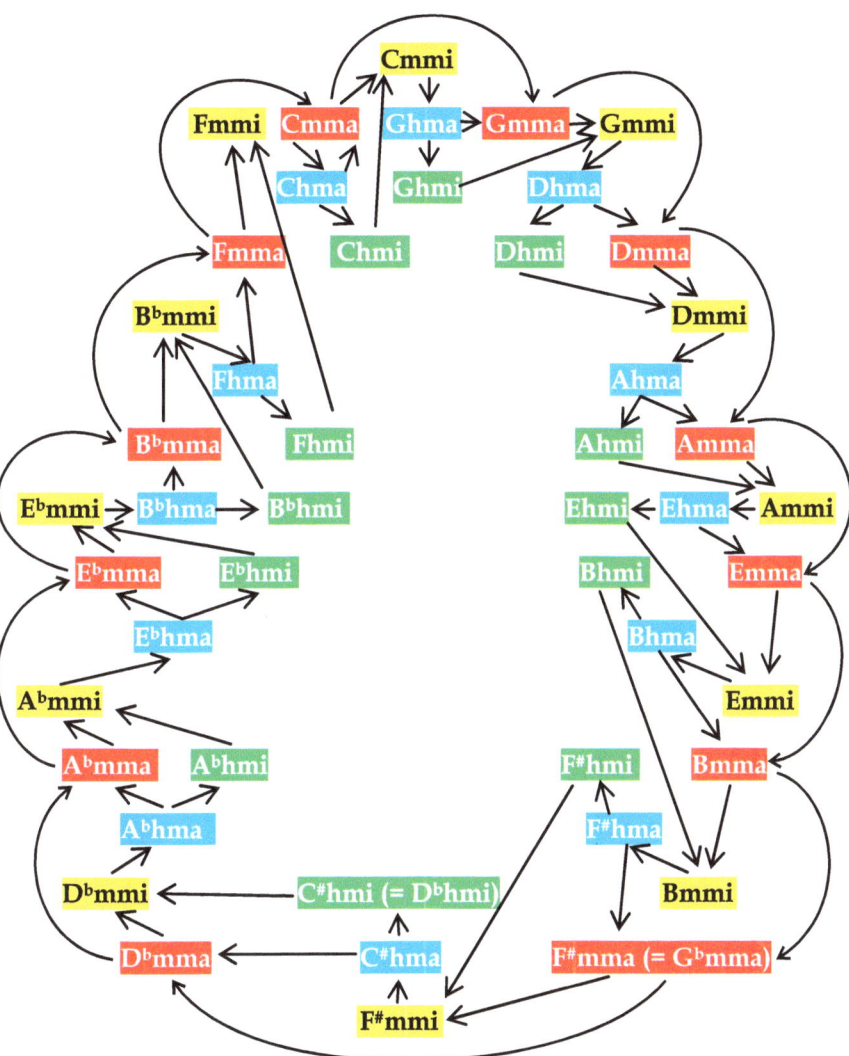

The curved arrows indicate the classical 5th-circle of the mma-scales.

Here are all the scales again, in a (double) row. In the brackets I have listed the notes by which the scales differ from **Cmma:**

Gmma(F#)

Cmmi(E♭) – Ghma(E♭, F#) – Ghmi(E♭, B♭, F#) – Gmmi(B♭, F#) –

Dmma(F#, C#)   Amma(F#, C#, G#)

- Dhma(B♭, F#, C#) – Dhmi(F#, C#) – Dmmi(C#) – Ahma(C#, G#) – Ahmi(G#) – Ammi(F#, G#)

Emma(F#, C#, G#, D#)

- Ehma(F#, G#, C#) – Ehmi (F#, D#) – Emmi(F#, C#, D#) –

Bmma(F#, C#, G#, D#, A#)

- Bhma(F#, C#, D#, A#) – Bhmi(F#, C#, A#) – Bmmi(F#, C#, G#, A#) –

F#mma(F#, C#, G#, D#, A#, E#)

- F#hma(F#, C#, G#, A#, E#) – F#hmi(F#, C#, G#, E#) - F#mmi(F#, C#, G#, D#, E#) –

(C#mma(F#, C#, G#, D#, A#, E#, B#)) = D♭mma(B♭, E♭, A♭, D♭, G♭)

- C#hma(F#, C#, G#, D#, E#, B#) - C#hmi(F#, C#, G#, D#, B#) (= D♭hmi(F♭, B♭♭, E♭, A♭, D♭, G♭)) - D♭mmi(F♭,

A♭mma(B♭, E♭, A♭, D♭)

B♭, E♭, A♭, D♭, G♭) - A♭hma(F♭, B♭, E♭, A♭, D♭) – A♭hmi(C♭ F♭, B♭, E♭, A♭, D♭) – A♭mmi(C♭, B♭,

E♭mma(B♭, E♭, A♭)

E♭, A♭, D♭) - E♭hma(C♭, B♭, E♭, A♭) – E♭hmi(G♭, C♭, B♭, E♭, A♭) – E♭mmi(G♭, B♭, E♭, A♭) –

B♭mma(B♭, E♭)

- B♭hma(G♭, B♭, E♭) - B♭hmi(D♭, G♭, B♭, E♭) - B♭mmi(D♭, B♭, E♭) –

Fmma(B♭)   Cmma( )

- Fhma(D♭, B♭) - Fhmi(A♭, D♭, B♭) – Fmmi(A♭, B♭) – Chma(A♭) – Chmi(E♭, A♭) - Cmmi(E♭)